MW00881410

Fortress

of the

Muslim

Hisnul Muslim – حصن المسلم

Invocations and Supplications from the Quran and the Sunnah

By Said Ibn Ali Al-Qahtani

بسم الله الرحمن الرحيم

In the name of Allah, Most Gracious, Most Merciful

TRANSLITERATIONS

أَ	A	about.
آ	<u>a</u>	c<u>a</u>t.
أُ	o	on.
ع	AA	say "a" twice distinctly with an open mouth.
ب	b	box.
د	d	door.
ض	<u>d</u>	heavy "d" sound (open jaw but keep lips tightly round).
ي	ee	feet.
ف	f	fish.
غ	gh	the sound you make when gargling.
إِ	I	ink.
ج	j	jar.
ك	k	kit.
خ	kh	gravely "h" sound.
ل	l	look.
م	m	man.
ن	n	nurse.
و	oo	pool.
ق	q	queen ("k" sound made in back of throat).
ر	r	rabbit (rolled "r" sound similar to Spanish "r").
ش	sh	ship.

س	s	sea.
ص	<u>s</u>	heavy "s" sound.
ت	t	tan.
ط	<u>t</u>	heavy " t" sound.
ث	th	think.
ذ	<u>th</u>	the.
ظ	<u>*th*</u>	"th" sound as in "the" but heavier.
ضّة	u	put.
ؤ	w	water.
ء	/	pronounce the letter before but cut it short by stopping suddenly.
ئ	y	yarn.
ز	z	zebra.

(-) is to make some words easier to read.
Bold letters are silent. i.e w: write.

1. WHEN WAKING UP

(1)

الحَمْدُ لِلّٰهِ الّذي أَحْيانا بَعْدَ ما أَماتَنا وَإليه النُّشور.

Alhamdu lillahil-lathee ahyana baAAda ma amatana wa-ilayhin-nushoor.

'All praise is for Allah who gave us life after having taken it from us and unto Him is the resurrection.'

(2)

The Prophet ﷺ said: 'Whoever awakes at night and then says:

لا إلهَ إلاّ اللّٰهُ وَحْدَهُ لا شَريكَ لهُ، لهُ المُلكُ ولهُ الحَمـد، وهوَ على كلِّ شيءٍ قدير، سُبْحانَ اللّٰهِ، والحَمْدُ لله ، ولا إلهَ إلاّ اللّٰهُ واللّٰهُ أَكبَر، وَلا حَوْلَ وَلا قوّة إلاّ بِاللّٰهِ العليِّ العظيم.

La ilaha illal-lahu wahdahu la shareeka lah, lahul-mulku walahul-hamd, wahuwa AAala kulli shay-in qadeer, subhanal-lah, walhamdu lillah, wala ilaha illal-lah wallahu akbar, wala hawla wala quwwata illa billahil-AAaliyyil AAatheem.

'None has the right to be worshipped except Allah, alone without associate, to Him belongs sovereignty and praise and He is over all things wholly capable. How perfect Allah is, and all praise is for Allah, and none has the right to be worshipped except Allah, Allah is the greatest and there is no power nor might except with Allah, The Most High, The Supreme.
...and then supplicates:

رَبِّ اغْفِرْ لي.

Rabbigh-fir lee

'O my Lord forgive me.'
…will be forgiven'
Al-Waleed said, "or he ﷺ said:
'and then asks, he will be answered. If he then performs ablution and prays, his prayer will be accepted'."

(3)

الحمدُ للهِ الذي عافاني في جَسَدي وَرَدّ عَليّ روحي وَأَذِنَ لي بِذِكْرِه .

Alhamdu lillahil-lathee AAafanee fee jasadee waradda AAalayya roohee wa-athina lee bithikrih.

'All praise is for Allah who restored to me my health and returned my soul and has allowed me to remember Him.'

(4)

﴿ إِنّ في خَلْقِ السّمَوَاتِ وَالأرْضِ واخْتِلافِ اللّيلِ والنّهارِ لآياتٍ لأُولي الألباب ...﴾

[سورة آل عمران 190-200]

❨Inna fee khalqi alssamawati waal-ardi wa-ikhtilafi allayli wa-alnnahari la-ayatin li-olee al-albab...❩

[From Verse 190 till the end of the chapter 3 Ali AAimran]

2. SUPPLICATION WHEN WEARING A GARMENT

(5)

الحمدُ للهِ الّذي كَساني هذا (الثّوب) وَرَزَقنيهِ مِنْ غَيرِ حَولٍ مِنّي وَلا قـوّة .

Alhamdu lillahil-lathee kasanee hatha (aththawb) warazaqaneehi min ghayri hawlin minnee wala quwwah.

'All Praise is for Allah who has clothed me with this garment and provided it for me, with no power nor might from myself.'

3. SUPPLICATION SAID WHEN WEARING A NEW GARMENT

(6)

اللّهُمَّ لَكَ الحَمْدُ أَنْتَ كَسَوْتَنيهِ، أَسْأَلُكَ مِنْ خَيرِهِ وَخَيْرِ مَا صُنِعَ لَه، وَأَعوذُ بِكَ مِنْ شَرِّهِ وَشَرِّ مَا صُنِعَ لَهُ.

Allahumma lakal-hamdu anta kasawtaneeh, as-aluka min khayrihi wakhayri ma suniAAa lah, wa-aAAoothu bika min sharrihi washarri ma suniAAa lah.

'O Allah, for You is all praise, You have clothed me with it (i.e. the garment), I ask You for the good of it and the good for which it was made, and I seek refuge with You from the evil of it and the evil for which it was made.'

4. SUPPLICATION SAID TO SOMEONE WEARING A NEW GARMENT

(7)

تُبْلي وَيُخْلِفُ اللهُ تَعَالى .

Tublee wayukhliful-lahu taAAala.

'May you wear it out and Allah تعالى replace it (with another).'

The intended meaning: A supplication for long life.

(8)

اِلبَس جَديداً وَعِش حَميداً وَمُت شَهيداً

Ilbas jadeedan waAAaish hameedan wamut shaheedan.

'Wear anew, live commendably and die a *shaheed*.'

-shaheed: One who dies fighting the kuffar in order to make the word of Allah superior or in defense of Islam. It also has other meanings found in the Sunnah such as: the one who dies defending his life, wealth or family; the woman who passes away due to childbirth; one who drowns…etc.

5. BEFORE UNDRESSING

(9)

بِسْمِ الله .

Bismil-lah

'In the name of Allah.'

6. BEFORE ENTERING THE TOILET

(10)

(بِسْمِ الله) اللّهُمَّ إِنِّي أَعوذُ بِكَ مِنَ الخُبْثِ والخَبائِث .

(Bismil-lah) allahumma innee aAAoothu bika minal-khubthi wal-khaba-ith

'(In the name of All<u>a</u>h). O All<u>a</u>h, I take refuge with you from all evil and evil-doers.'

7. AFTER LEAVING THE TOILET
(11)

غُفْرانَك .

Ghufr<u>a</u>nak

'I ask You (All<u>a</u>h) for forgiveness.'

8. WHEN STARTING ABLUTION
(12)

بِسْمِ الله .

Bismil-l<u>a</u>h

'In the name of All<u>a</u>h.'

9. UPON COMPLETING THE ABLUTION
(13)

أَشْهَدُ أَنْ لا إِلَهَ إِلاَّ اللهُ وَحْدَهُ لا شَرِيكَ لَهُ وَأَشْهَدُ أَنَّ مُحَمَّداً عَبْدُهُ وَرَسولُه.

Ashhadu an l<u>a</u> il<u>a</u>ha illal-l<u>a</u>hu wa<u>h</u>dahu l<u>a</u> shareeka lah, wa-ashhadu anna Mu<u>h</u>ammadan AAabduhu warasooluh.

'I bear witness that none has the right to be worshipped except All<u>a</u>h, alone without partner, and I bear witness that Mu<u>h</u>ammad is His slave and Messenger.'

اللّهُـمَّ اجْعَلنـي مِنَ التَّـوّابينَ وَاجْعَـلْني مِنَ المتَطَهّـرين .

Allahummaj- AAalnee minat-tawwabeena waj-
AAalnee minal- mutatahhireen.

'O Allah, make me of those who return to You often
in repentance and make me of those who remain
clean and pure.'

(15)

سُبْحـانَكَ اللّهُـمَّ وَبِحَمدِك أَشْهَدُ أَنْ لا إِلهَ إِلاّ أَنْتَ أَسْتَغْفِرُكَ
وَأَتوبُ إِلَـيْك .

Subhanakal-lahumma wabihamdika ashhadu an la
ilaha illa anta astaghfiruka wa-atoobu ilayk.

'How perfect You are O Allah, and I praise You, I
bear witness that none has the right to be
worshipped except You, I seek Your forgiveness and
turn in repentance to You.'

10. WHEN LEAVING THE HOME

(16)

بِسْمِ اللهِ ، تَوَكَّلْتُ عَلى اللهِ وَلا حَوْلَ وَلا قُوَّةَ إِلاّ بِاللهِ .

Bismil-lah, tawakkaltu AAalal-lah, wala hawla
wala quwwata illa billah.

'In the name of Allah, I place my trust in Allah, and
there is no might nor power except with Allah.'

(17)

اللّهُمَّ إِنِّي أَعُوذُ بِكَ أَنْ أَضِلَّ أَوْ أُضَلَّ أَوْ أُضَلَّ، أَوْ أَزِلَّ أَوْ أُزَلَّ، أَوْ أَظْلِمَ أَوْ أُظْلَمَ، أَوْ أَجْهَلَ أَوْ يُجْهَلَ عَلَيَّ .

Allahumma innee aAAoothu bika an adilla aw odal, aw azilla aw ozall, aw athlima aw othlam, aw ajhala aw yujhala AAalay.

'O Allah, I take refuge with You lest I should stray or be led astray, or slip or be tripped, or oppress or be oppressed, or behave foolishly or be treated foolishly.'

-slip: i.e. to commit a sin unintentionally

11. UPON ENTERING THE HOME

(18)

بِسْمِ اللهِ وَلَجْنا، وَبِسْمِ اللهِ خَرَجْنا، وَعَلَى رَبِّنا تَوَكَّلْنا .

Bismil-lahi walajna, wabismil-lahi kharajna, waAAala rabbina tawakkalna.

'In the name of Allah we enter and in the name of Allah we leave, and upon our Lord we place our trust.'

12. SUPPLICATION WHEN GOING TO THE MOSQUE

(19)

اللّهُمَّ اجْعَلْ في قَلْبي نورا ، وَفي لِساني نورا، وَاجْعَلْ في سَمْعي نورا، وَاجْعَلْ في بَصَري نورا، وَاجْعَلْ مِنْ خَلْفي نورا، وَمِنْ

أَمامـي نورا، وَاجْعَـلْ مِنْ فَوْقـي نورا ، وَمِن تَحْتـي نورا .اللَّهُـمَّ
أَعْطِنـي نورا .

Allahumma ijAAal fee qalbee noora, wafee lisanee
noora, wajAAal fee samAAee noora,wajAAal fee
basaree noora, wajAAal min khalfee noora, wamin
amamee noora ,wajAAal min fawqee noora, wamin
tahtee noora, allahumma aAAtinee noora.

'O Allah, place within my heart light, and upon my
tongue light, and within my ears light, and within
my eyes light, and place behind me light and in front
of me light and above me light and beneath me light.
O Allah, bestow upon me light.'

13. UPON ENTERING THE MOSQUE

(20)

أَعوذُ باللهِ العَظيـمِ وَبِوَجْهِـهِ الكَريـمِ وَسُلْطانِه القَديـم مِنَ
الشَّيْطانِ الرَّجيمِ، بِسـمِ اللهِ، وَالصَّلاةُ وَالسَّلامُ عَلى رَسولِ اللهِ،
اللَّهُـمَّ افْتَـحْ لي أَبْوابَ رَحْمَتِـك .

aAAoothu   billahil-AAatheem   wabiwajhihil-
kareem   wasultanihil-qadeem   minash-shaytanir-
rajeem, bismil-lah, wassalatu wassalamu AAala
rasoolil-lah , allahumma iftah lee abwaba rahmatik.

'I take refuge with Allah, The Supreme and with His
Noble Face, and His eternal authority from the
accursed devil. In the name of Allah, and prayers and
peace be upon the Messenger of Allah. O Allah,
open the gates of Your mercy for me.'

14. UPON LEAVING THE MOSQUE

(21)

بِسمِ اللهِ وَالصّلاةُ وَالسّلامُ عَلى رَسولِ اللهِ، اللّهُمَّ إنّي أَسأَلُكَ مِنْ فَضْلِكَ، اللّهُمَّ اعصِمْني مِنَ الشّيْطانِ الرّجيمِ.

Bismil-l**a**h wa**ss**al**a**tu wassal**a**mu AAal**a** rasoolil-l**a**h, all**a**humma innee as-aluka min fa**d**lik, all**a**humma iAA**s**imnee minash-shay**t**anir-rajeem.

'In the name of All**a**h, and prayers and peace be upon the Messenger of All**a**h. O All**a**h, I ask You from Your favour. O All**a**h, guard me from the accursed devil.'

15. SUPPLICATIONS RELATED TO THE A**TH**AN (THE CALL TO PRAYER)

(22)

*'One repeats just as the mu-a**thth**in (one who calls to prayer) says, except when he says:*

حَـيَّ عَلى الصّلاةِ (أَو) حَـيَّ عَلى الْفَـلاحِ.

Hayya AAala**s**-**s**al**a**h (or) **h**ayya AAalal-fal**a**h

'come to prayer, come to success'
instead, one should say:

لا حَـوْلَ وُلا قُوَةَ إلاّ بِاللهِ.

L**a h**awla wal**a** quwwata ill**a** bill**a**h.

'There is no might nor power except with All**a**h.'

(23)

*Immediately following the declaration of faith called by the mu-a**thth**in, one says:*

وَأَنا أَشْـهَدُ أَنْ لا إِلهَ إِلاّ اللّٰهُ وَحْدَهُ لا شَـريكَ لَه ، وَأَنَّ مُحَمَّداً عَبْدُهُ وَرَسولُه ، رَضيـتُ بِاللّٰهِ رَبّاً ، وَبِمُحَمَّـدٍ رَسولاً وَبِالإِسْلام ديناً .

Wa-ana ashhadu an la ilaha illal-lahu wahdahu la shareeka lah, wa-anna Muhammadan AAabduhu warasooluh, radeetu billahi rabban wabimuhammadin rasoolan wabil-islami deena.

'And I too bear witness that none has the right to be worshipped except Allah, alone, without partner, and that Muhammad is His salve and Messenger. I am pleased with Allah as a Lord, and Muhammad as a Messenger and Islam as a religion.'

(24)

'One should then send prayers on the Prophet ﷺ after answering the call of the mu-aththin'

(25)

اللّهُمَّ رَبَّ هَذِهِ الدّعْوَةِ التّامَّةِ وَالصّلاةِ القَائِمَة آتِ مُحَمَّداً الوَسيلةَ وَالْفَضيلةَ وَابْعَثْه مَقاماً مَحْموداً الَّذي وَعَدْتَه إِنَّكَ لا تُخْلِفُ الميعاد.

Allahumma rabba hathihid-daAAwatit-tammah, wassalatil-qa-imah ati Muhammadan alwaseelata wal-fadeelah, wabAAath-hu maqaman mahmoodan allathee waAAadtah, innaka la tukhliful-meeAAad.

'O Allah, Owner of this perfect call and Owner of this prayer to be performed, bestow upon Muhammad *al-*

---

waseelah and *al-fadeelah* and send him upon a praised platform which You have promised him. Verily, You never fail in Your promise.'

-*al-waseelah*: A station in paradise.
-*al-fadeelah*: A rank above the rest of creation.
-praised platform: One in which all of creation will praise him on, in order to bring about the account quickly and be relieved from the lengthy standing *or* the role of intercession.

(26)
One should also supplicate for himself during the time between the athan and the iqamah as supplication at such time is not rejected.

16. SUPPLICATION AT THE START OF THE PRAYER (AFTER TAKBEER)

(27)

اللّهُمَّ باعِدْ بَيْنِي وَبَيْنَ خَطايايَ كَمَا باعَدْتَ بَيْنَ المَشْرِقِ وَالمَغْرِبْ ، اللّهُمَّ نَقِّنِي مِنْ خَطايايَ كَمَا يُنَقَّى الثَّوْبُ الأَبْيَضُ مِنَ الدَّنَسْ ، اللّهُمَّ اغْسِلْنِي مِنْ خَطايايَ بِالثَّلجِ وَالماءِ وَالْبَرَدْ.

Allahumma baAAid baynee wabayna khatayaya kama baAAadta baynal-mashriqi walmaghrib, allahumma naqqinee min khatayaya kama yunaqqath-thawbul-abyadu minad-danas, allahummagh-silnee min khatayaya biththalji walma/i walbarad.

'O Allah, distance me from my sins just as You have distanced The East from The West, O Allah, purify me of my sins as a white robe is purified of filth, O Allah, cleanse me of my sins with snow, water, and ice.'

(28)

سُبْحانَكَ اللّهُمَّ وَبِحَمْدِكَ وَتَبارَكَ اسْمُكَ وَتَعالى جَدُّكَ وَلا إلهَ غَيْرُك .

Subhanakal-lahumma wabihamdika watabarakas-muka wataAAala jadduka wala ilaha ghayruk.

'How perfect You are O Allah, and I praise You. Blessed be Your name, and lofty is Your position and none has the right to be worshipped except You.'

(29)

وَجَّهْتُ وَجْهِيَ لِلَّذي فَطَرَ السَّمواتِ والأرْضَ حَنيفاً وَما أنا مِنَ المُشْرِكين ، إنَّ صَلاتي ، وَنُسُكي ، وَمَحْيايَ ، وَمَماتي لله رَبِّ العالَمين ، لا شَريكَ لَهُ وَبِذلكَ أُمِرْتُ وَأَنا مِنَ المُسْلِمين . اللّهُمَّ أَنْتَ المَلِكُ لا إلهَ إلاّ أَنْتَ ،أَنْتَ رَبّي وَأَنا عَبْدُك ، ظَلَمْتُ نَفْسي وَاعْتَرَفْتُ بِذَنْبي فَاغْفِرْ لي ذُنوبي جَميعاً إنَّهُ لا يَغْفِرُ الذُّنوبَ إلاّ أَنْت .وَاهْدِني لأَحْسَنِ الأَخْلاقِ لا يَهْدي لأَحْسَنِها إلاّ أَنْت ، وَاصْرِف عَنّي سَيِّئَها ، لا يَصْرِفُ عَنّي سَيِّئَها إلاّ أَنْت ، لَبَّيْكَ وَسَعْدَيْك ، والخَيْرُ كُلُّهُ بِيَدَيْك ،

وَالشَّرُّ لَيْسَ إِلَيْكَ ، أَنا بِكَ وَإِلَيْكَ ، تَبَارَكْتَ وَتَعالَيْتَ أَسْتَغْفِرُكَ وَأَتوبُ إِلَيْكَ .

Wajjahtu wajhiya lillathee fataras-samawati wal-arda haneefan wama ana minal-mushrikeen, inna salatee wanusukee wamahyaya wamamatee lillahi rabbil-AAalameen, la shareeka lahu wabithalika omirtu wa-ana minal-muslimeen. Allahumma antal-maliku la ilaha illa ant. anta rabbee wa-ana AAabduk, thalamtu nafsee waAAtaraftu bithanbee faghfir lee thunoobee jameeAAan innahu la yaghfiruth-thunooba illa ant.wahdinee li-ahsanil-akhlaqi la yahdee li-ahsaniha illa ant, wasrif AAannee sayyi-aha la yasrifu AAannee sayyi-aha illa ant, labbayka wasaAAdayk,walkhayru kulluhu biyadayk, washsharru laysa ilayk, ana bika wa-ilayk, tabarakta wataAAalayt, astaghfiruka wa-atoobu ilayk.

'I have turned my face sincerely towards He who has brought forth the heavens and the Earth and I am not of those who associate (others with Allah). Indeed my prayer, my sacrifice, my life and my death are for Allah, Lord of the worlds, no partner has He, with this I am commanded and I am of the Muslims. O Allah, You are the Sovereign, none has the right to be worshipped except You. You are my Lord and I am Your servant, I have wronged my own soul and have acknowledged my sin, so forgive me all my sins for no one forgives sins except You. Guide me to the best of characters for none can guide to it other than You, and deliver me from the worst of characters for none can deliver me from it other than You. Here I am, in answer to Your call, happy to serve you. All good is within Your hands and evil does not stem from You. I exist by your will and will return to you. Blessed and High are You, I seek Your forgiveness and repent unto You.'

Allah does not create pure evil which does not have any good or contain any benefit, wisdom or mercy at all, nor does He punish anyone without having commited a sin. Something can be good in terms of its creation when viewed in a particular perspective and at the same time be evil when viewed in another way. Allah created the devil and by him, He tests His servants, so there are those who hate the devil, fight him and his way and they stand at enmity towards him and his followers and there are others who are at allegiance with the devil and follow his steps. So evil exists in His creatures by His will and wisdom, not in His actions or act of creating.

(30)

اللّهُمَّ رَبَّ جِبْرائِيل ، وَمِيكـائِيل ، وَإِسْرافِيل، فاطِرَ السَّمواتِ وَالأَرْض ، عالِمَ الغَيْبِ وَالشَّهـادَةِ أَنْتَ تَحْكُمُ بَيْنَ عِبادِكَ فيمـا كانوا فيهِ يَخْتَلِفون. اهدِني لِمـا اخْتُلِفَ فيهِ مِنَ الحَقِّ بِإِذْنِك ، إِنَّكَ تَهدي مَنْ تَشاءُ إلى صِراطٍ مُسْتَقيم .

Allahumma rabba jibra-eel, wameeka-eel, wa-israfeel fatiras-samawati walard, AAalimal-ghaybi washshahadah, anta tahkumu bayna AAibadika feema kanoo feehi yakhtalifoon. ihdinee limakh-tulifa feehi minal-haqqi bi-ithnik, innaka tahdee man tasha-o ila siratin mustaqeem.

'O All<u>a</u>h, Lord of *Jibra-eel*, *Meeka-eel* and *Isr<u>a</u>feel* (great angles), Creator of the heavens and the Earth, Knower of the seen and the unseen. You are the arbitrator between Your servants in that which they have disputed. Guide me to the truth by Your leave, in that which they have differed, for verily You guide whom You will to a straight path.'

(31)

اللّٰهُ أَكْبَرُ كَبِيرا ، اللّٰهُ أَكْبَرُ كَبِيرا ، اللّٰهُ أَكْبَرُ كَبِيرا ، وَالْحَمْدُ لِلّٰهِ كَثيرا ، وَالْحَمْدُ لِلّٰهِ كَثيرا ، وَالْحَمْدُ لِلّٰهِ كَثيرا ، وَسُبْحانَ اللّٰهِ بكْرَةً وَأَصيلا . (ثَلاثاً)

أَعوذُ بِاللّٰهِ مِنَ الشَّيْطانِ مِنْ نَفْخِهِ وَنَفْثِهِ وَهَمْزه .

Allahu akbaru kabeera, Allahu akbaru kabeera, Allahu akbaru kabeera, walhamdu lillahi katheera, walhamdu lillahi katheera, walhamdu lillahi katheera, wasubhanal-lahi bukratan wa-aseela. (three times)

aAAoothu billahi minash-shaytani min nafkhihi wanafthihi wahamzih.

'Allah is Most Great, Allah is Most Great, Allah is Most Great, much praise is for Allah, much praise is for Allah, much praise is for Allah, and I declare the perfection of Allah in the early morning and in the late afternoon.'(three times)

'I take refuge with Allah from the devil, from his pride, his poetry and his madness.'

The prophet ﷺ would say (as an opening supplication in prayer) when rising from sleep to perform prayers during the night:

اللّٰهُمَّ لَكَ الْحَمْدُ أَنْتَ نورُ السَّمواتِ والأَرْضِ وَمَنْ فيهِنَّ ، وَلَكَ الْحَمْدُ أَنْتَ قَيِّمُ السَّمواتِ والأَرْضِ وَمَنْ فيهِنَّ ، [وَلَكَ الْحَمْدُ أَنْتَ رَبُّ السَّمواتِ والأَرْضِ وَمَنْ فيهِنَّ] [وَلَكَ الْحَمْدُ لَكَ مُلْكُ السَّمواتِ والأَرْضِ وَمَنْ فيهِنَّ] [وَلَكَ الْحَمْدُ أَنْتَ مَلِكُ السَّمواتِ والأَرْضِ] [وَلَكَ الْحَمْدُ] [أَنْتَ الْحَقّ وَوَعْدُكَ الْحَقّ ، وَقَوْلُكَ الْحَقّ ، وَلِقاؤُكَ الْحَقّ ، والْجَنَّةُحَقّ ، والنّارُ حَقّ ، والنَّبِيّونَ حَقّ ، وَمحَمَّدٌ ﷺ حَقّ ، والسّاعَةُحَقّ] [اللّٰهُمَّ لَكَ أَسْلَمْت ، وَعَلَيْكَ تَوَكَّلْت ، وَبِكَ آمَنْت ، وَإِلَيْكَ أَنَبْت ، وَبِكَ خاصَمْت ، وَإِلَيْكَ حاكَمْت . فاغْفِرْ لي ما قَدَّمْتُ ، وَما أَخَّرْت ، وَما أَسْرَرْت ، وَما أَعْلَنْت] [أَنْتَ الْمُقَدِّمُ وَأَنْتَ الْمُؤَخِّر ، لا إِلٰهَ إِلّا أَنْت] [أَنْتَ إِلٰهِي لا إِلٰهَ إِلّا أَنْت].

Allahumma lakal-hamd anta noorus-samawati wal-ardi waman feehin, walakal-hamd, anta qayyimus-samawati walardi waman feehin, [walakal-hamd, anta rabbus-samawati walardi waman feehin], [walakal-hamd, laka mulkus-samawati walardi waman feehin] [walakal-hamd, anta malikus-samawati walard] [walakal-hamd] [antal-haq, wawaAAdukal-haq, waqawlukal-haq, waliqa-okal-

haq, waljannatu haq wannaru haq, wannabiyyoona haq, wa Muhammadun ﷺ haq, wassaAAatu haq] [allahumma laka aslamt, waAAalayka tawakkalt, wabika amant, wa-ilayka anabt, wabika khasamt, wa-ilayka hakamt, faghfir lee ma qaddamt, wama akhkhart, wama asrart, wama aAAlant] [antal-muqaddim, wa-antal-mu-akhkhir, la ilaha illa ant] [anta ilahee la ilaha illa ant .

'O Allah, to You belongs all praise, You are the Light of the heavens and the Earth and all that is within them. To You belongs all praise, You are the Sustainer of the heavens and the Earth and all that is within them. To You belongs all praise. You are Lord of the heavens and the Earth and all that is within them. To You belongs all praise and the kingdom of the heavens and the Earth and all that is within them. To You belongs all praise, You are the King of the heavens and the Earth and to You belongs all praise. You are The Truth, Your promise is true, your Word is true, and the Day in which we will encounter You is true, the Garden of Paradise is true and the Fire is true, and the Prophets are true, Muhammad ﷺ is true and the Final Hour is true. O Allah, unto You I have submitted, and upon You I have relied, and in You I have believed, and to You I have turned in repentance, and over You I have disputed, and to You I have turned for judgment. So forgive me for what has come to pass of my sins and what will come to pass, and what I have hidden and what I have made public. You are *Al-Muqaddim* and *Al-Mu-akhkhir*. None has the right to be worshipped except You, You are my Deity, none has the right to be worshipped except You.'

Meaning of *Al-Muqaddim* **and** *Al-Mu-akhkhir*: All<u>a</u>h puts forward and favours whom He wills from amongst His creation just as He defers and holds back whom He wills in accordance to His wisdom. E.g. Favouring man over the rest of creation, favouring the Prophets over the rest of mankind, favouring Mu<u>h</u>ammad ﷺ over all the Prophets and Messengers…etc.

17. WHILE BOWING IN PRAYER (RUKOOAA)

(33)

سُبْحانَ رَبِّيَ الْعَظِيم . (ثلاثاً)

Sub<u>h</u>ana rabbiyal-AAa*th***eem** (three times)

'How perfect my Lord is, The Supreme.' (three times)

(34)

سُبْحانَكَ اللّهُمَّ رَبَّنا وَبِحَمْدِك ، اللّهُمَّ اغْفِرْ لي .

Sub<u>h</u>anakal-l<u>a</u>humma rabban<u>a</u> wabi<u>h</u>amdik, all<u>a</u>hummagh-fir lee

'How perfect You are O All<u>a</u>h, our Lord and I praise You. O All<u>a</u>h, forgive me.'

(35)

سُبّوحٌ قُدّوس ، رَبُّ الملائِكَةِ وَالرُّوح .

Subboo<u>h</u>un quddoos, rabbul-mal<u>a</u>-ikati warroo<u>h</u>.

'Perfect and Holy (He is), Lord of the angles and the *Roo<u>h</u>* (i.e. Jibr<u>a</u>-eel).'

22

(36)

اللّهُمَّ لَكَ رَكَعْتُ وَبِكَ آمَنْت ، ولَكَ أَسْلَمْت ، خَشَعَ لَكَ سَمْعي ، وَبَصَري ، وَمُخِّي ، وَعَظْمي ، وَعَصَبي ، وَما استَقَلَّ بِهِ قَدَمي .

Alla̲humma laka rakaAAt, wabika a̲mant, walaka aslamt, khashaAAa laka samAAee, waba̲saree, wamukhkhee, waAAa̲thmee, waAAa̲sabee, wamas-taqalla bihi qadamee.

'O Alla̲h, unto You I have bowed, and in You I have believed, and to You I have submitted. My hearing, sight, mind, bones, tendons and what my feet carry are humbled before You.'

(37)

سُبْحانَ ذي الجَبَروت ، والمَلَكوت ، وَالكِبْرِياء ، وَالْعَظَمَه .

Subha̲na t̲hil-jabaroot, walmalakoot, walkibriya̲/, walAAa̲thamah.

'How perfect He is, The Possessor of total power, sovereignty, magnificence and grandeur.'

18. UPON RISING FROM THE BOWING POSITION

(38)

سَمِعَ اللهُ لِمَنْ حَمِدَه .

SamiAAal-la̲hu liman h̲amidah.

'May Alla̲h answer he who praises Him.'

This supplication is to be made *while* rising.

(39)

رَبَّنا وَلَكَ الحَمْدُ حَمْداً كَثِيراً طَيِّباً مُبارَكاً فيه .

Rabbana walakal-ḥamdu ḥamdan katheeran ṭayyiban mubᾱrakan feeh.

'Our Lord, for You is all praise, an abundant beautiful blessed praise.'

(40)

مِلْءَ السَّمـواتِ وَمِلْءَ الأَرْضِ ، وَما بَيْـنَهُمـا ، وَمِلْءَ ما شِئْـتَ مِنْ شَيءٍ بَعْدُ . أَهلَ الثَّناءِ والمَجْدُ ، أَحَقُّ ما قالَ العَبْدُ ، وَكُلُّنا لَكَ عَبْدُ . اللّهُمَّ لا مانِعَ لِما أَعْطَيْت ، وَلا مُعْطِيَ لِما مَنَعْت ، وَلا يَنْفَعُ ذا الجَدِّ مِنْكَ الجَد .

Mil-as-samᾱwati wamil-al-arḍ, wama baynahumᾱ, wamil/a mᾱ shi/ta min shay-in baAAd, ahlath-thanᾱ-i walmajd, aḥaqqu mᾱ qalal-AAabd, wakullunᾱ laka AAabd. Allᾱhumma la maniAAa limᾱ aAAṭayt, walᾱ muAAṭiya limᾱ manaAAt, walᾱ yanfaAAu thal-jaddi minkal-jad.

'The heavens and the Earth and all between them abound with Your praises, and all that You will abounds with Your praises. O Possessor of praise and majesty, the truest thing a slave has said (of You) and we are all Your slaves. O Allᾱh, none can prevent what You have willed to bestow and none can bestow what You have willed to prevent, and no wealth or majesty can benefit anyone, as from You is all wealth and majesty.'

-This supplication is made optionally only in conjunction with the previous one.

19. SUPPLICATION WHILST PROSTRATING (SUJOOD)

(41)

سُبْحانَ رَبِّيَ الأَعْلى . (ثلاثاً)

Subhana rabbiyal-aAAla. (three times)

'How perfect my Lord is, The Most High.'(three times)

(42)

سُبْحانَكَ اللّهُمَّ رَبَّنا وَبِحَمْدِكَ ، اللّهُمَّ اغْفِرْ لي .

Subhanakal-lahumma rabbana wabihamdik, allahummagh- fir lee.

'How perfect You are O Allah, our Lord, and I praise You. O Allah, forgive me.'

(43)

سُبّوحٌ قُدّوس، رَبُّ الملائِكَةِ وَالرُّوح .

Subbohoon quddos, rabbul-mala-ikati warrooh.

'Perfect and Holy (He is), Lord of the angles and the *Rooh* (i.e. Jibra-eel).'

(44)

اللّهُمَّ لَكَ سَجَدْتُ وَبِكَ آمَنْت ، وَلَكَ أَسْلَمْت ، سَجَدَ وَجْهي لِلَّذي خَلَقَهُ وَصَوَّرَهُ وَشَقَّ سَمْعَهُ وَبَصَرَه ، تَبـارَكَ اللّهُ أَحْسنُ الخـالِقيـن.

Allahumma laka sajadt, wabika amant, walaka aslamt, sajada wajhee lillathee khalaqahu wasawwarahu washaqqa samAAahu wabasarahu, tabarakal-lahu ahsanul-khaliqeen.

'O Allah, unto You I have prostrated and in You I have believed, and unto You I have submitted. My face has prostrated before He Who created it and fashioned it, and brought forth its faculties of hearing and seeing. Blessed is Allah, the Best of creators.'

(45)

سُبْحانَ ذي الْجَبَروت ، والمَلَكوت ، والكِبْرِياء ، وَالعَظَمَه .

Subhana thil-jabaroot, walmalakoot, walkibriya/, walAAathamah.

'How perfect He is, The Possessor of total power, sovereignty, magnificence and grandeur.'

(46)

اللّهُمَّ اغْفِرْ لي ذَنْبي كُلَّه ، دِقَّهُ وَجِلَّه ، وَأَوَّلَهُ وَآخِرَه وَعَلانِيَّتَهُ وَسِرَّه .

Allahummagh-fir lee thanbee kullah, diqqahu wajillah, wa-awwalahu wa-akhirah, wa-AAalaniyyatahu wa-sirrah.

'O Allah, forgive me all of my sins, the small and great of them, the first and last of them, and the seen and hidden of them.'

(47)

اللّهُـمَّ إِنِّي أَعوذُ بِرِضاكَ مِنْ سَخَطِك ، وَبِمـعـافـاتِكَ مِنْ عُقوبَـتِك ، وَأَعوذُ بِكَ مِنْـك ، لا أُحْصي ثَناءً عَلَيْك ، أَنْـتَ كَما أَثْنَـيْتَ عَلى نَفْسـِك .

Alla<u>h</u>umma innee aAAoo<u>th</u>u biri<u>d</u>aka min sakha<u>t</u>ik, wa-bimuAA<u>a</u>fatika min AAuqoobatik, wa-aAAoo<u>th</u>u bika mink, <u>la</u> oh<u>s</u>ee than<u>a</u>-an AAalayk, anta kam<u>a</u> athnayta AAal<u>a</u> nafsik.

'O All<u>a</u>h, I take refuge within Your pleasure from Your displeasure and within Your pardon from Your punishment, and I take refuge in You from You. I cannot enumerate Your praise, You are as You have praised Yourself.'

20. SUPPLICATION BETWEEN THE TWO PROSTRATIONS

(48)

رَبِّ اغْفِرْ لي ، رَبِّ اغْفِرْ لي .

Rabbigh-fir lee, rabbigh-fir lee.

'My Lord forgive me, My Lord forgive me.'

(49)

اللّهُـمَّ اغْفِرْ لي ، وَارْحَمْني ، وَاهْدِني ، وَاجْبُرْني ، وَعافِني وَارْزُقْني وَارْفَعْني .

Alla<u>h</u>ummagh-fir lee, war<u>h</u>amnee, wahdinee, wajburnee, waAA<u>a</u>finee, warzuqnee warfaAAnee.

'O Allah, forgive me, have mercy upon me, guide me, enrich me, give me health, grant me sustenance and raise my rank.'

21. SUPPLICATION WHEN PROSTRATING DUE TO RECITATION OF THE QURAN

(50)

سَجَدَ وَجْهِي لِلَّذِي خَلَقَهُ وَصَوَّرَهُ وَشَقَّ سَمْعَهُ وَبَصَرَهُ بِحَوْلِهِ وَقُوَّتِهِ، ﴿تَبَارَكَ اللهُ أَحْسَنُ الْخَالِقِينَ﴾.

Sajada wajhee lillathee khalaqahu washaqqa samAAahu wabasarahu bihawlihi waquwwatih { tabaraka Allahu ahsanu alkhaliqeen}.

'My face fell prostrate before He who created it and brought forth its faculties of hearing and seeing by His might and power, "So Blessed is Allah, the best of creators". '

(51)

اللّٰهُمَّ اكْتُبْ لِي بِهَا عِنْدَكَ أَجْراً ، وَضَعْ عَنِّي بِهَا وِزْراً ، وَاجْعَلْها لِي عِنْدَكَ ذُخْراً ، وَتَقَبَّلْها مِنِّي كَمَا تَقَبَّلْتَها مِنْ عَبْدِكَ داود .

Allahummak-tub lee biha AAindaka ajra, wadaAA AAannee biha wizra, wajAAalha lee AAindaka thukhra, wataqabbalha minnee kama taqabbaltaha min AAabdika Dawood.

'O Allah, record for me a reward for this (prostration), and remove from me a sin. Save it for

me and accept it from me just as You had accepted it
from Your servant Dawood.'

22. THE TASHAHHUD

Tashahhud: what one says in the sitting position in
prayer

(52)

التَّحِيَّاتُ للهِ وَالصَّلَوَاتُ وَالطَّيِّبَاتُ ، السَّلَامُ عَلَيْكَ أَيُّهَا
النَّبِيُّ وَرَحْمَةُ اللهِ وَبَرَكَاتُهُ ، السَّلَامُ عَلَيْنَا وَعَلَى عِبَادِ كَ
الصَّالِحِينَ . أَشْهَدُ أَنْ لَا إِلَهَ إِلَّا اللهُ ، وَأَشْهَدُ أَنَّ مُحَمَّداً
عَبْدُهُ وَرَسُولُهُ .

**Attahiyyatu lillahi wassalawatu wattayyibat,
assalamu AAalayka ayyuhan-nabiyyu warahmatul-
lahi wabarakatuh, assalamu AAalayna waAAala
AAibadil-lahis-saliheen. Ash-hadu an la ilaha illal-
lah, wa-ashhadu anna Muhammadan AAabduhu
warasooluh.**

'*At-tahiyyat* are for Allah. All acts of worship and
good deeds are for Him. Peace and the mercy and
blessings of Allah be upon you O Prophet. Peace be
upon us and all of Allah's righteous servants. I bear
witness that none has the right to be worshipped
except Allah and I bear witness that Muhammad is
His slave and Messenger.'

-At-tahiyyat: all words which indicate the
glorification of Allah. His eternal existence, His
perfection and His sovereignty.

---

23. PRAYERS UPON THE PROPHET ﷺ AFTER THE TASHAHHUD

(53)

اللّهُمَّ صَلِّ عَلى مُحَمَّد، وَعَلى آلِ مُحَمَّد، كَما صَلَّيْتَ عَلى إِبْراهيمَ وَعَلى آلِ إِبْراهيمِ، إِنَّكَ حَميدٌ مَجيد ، اللّهُمَّ بارِكْ عَلى مُحَمَّد، وَعَلى آلِ مُحَمَّد، كَما بارَكْتَ عَلى إِبْراهيمَ وَعَلى آلِ إِبْراهيمِ، إِنَّكَ حَميدٌ مَجيد .

Alla̲humma s̲alli AAala̲ Muh̲ammad, wa-AAala̲ a̲li Muh̲ammad, kama s̲allayta AAala̲ Ibraheema wa-AAala̲ a̲li Ibraheem, innaka H̲ameedun Majeed, alla̲humma ba̲rik AAala̲ Muh̲ammad, wa-AAala̲ a̲li Muh̲ammad, kama ba̲rakta AAala̲ Ibraheema wa-AAala̲ a̲li Ibraheem, innaka H̲ameedun Majeed.

'O Alla̲h, send prayers upon Muh̲ammad and the followers of Muh̲ammad, just as You sent prayers upon Ibra̲heem and upon the followers of Ibra̲heem. Verily, You are full of praise and majesty. O Alla̲h, send blessings upon Moh̲ammad and upon the family of Muh̲ammad, just as You sent blessings upon Ibra̲heem and upon the family of Ibra̲heem. Verily, You are full of praise and majesty.'

-send prayers: praise and exalt him in the highest and superior of gatherings: that of the closest angels to Alla̲h.

-(a̲l) has been translated in it's broadest sense: some scholars are of the view that the meaning here is more specific and that it means: *his ﷺ followers from among his family.*

(54)

اللّهُمَّ صَلِّ عَلى مُحَمَّدٍ وَعَلى أَزْواجِهِ وَذُرِّيَّتِه، كَما صَلَّيْتَ عَلى آلِ إِبْراهيم . وَبارِكْ عَلى مُحَمَّدٍ وَعَلى أَزْواجِهِ وَذُرِّيَّتِه، كَما بارَكْتَ عَلى آلِ إِبْراهيم . إِنَّكَ حَميدٌ مَجيد .

Allahumma salli AAala Muhammad wa-AAala azwajihi wathurriyyatihi kama sallayta AAala ali Ibraheem, wabarik AAala Muhammad, wa-AAala azwajihi wathurriyyatih, kama barakta AAala ali Ibraheem. innaka Hameedun Majeed.

'O Allah, send prayers upon Muhammad and upon the wives and descendants of Muhammad, just as You sent prayers upon the family of Ibraheem, and send blessings upon Muhammad and upon the wives and descendants of Muhammad, just as You sent blessings upon the family of Ibraheem. Verily, You are full of praise and majesty.'

24. SUPPLICATION SAID AFTER THE LAST TASHAHHUD AND BEFORE SALAM

(55)

اللّهُمَّ إِنِّي أَعوذُ بِكَ مِنْ عَذابِ القَبْرِ، وَمِنْ عَذابِ جَهَنَّم، وَمِنْ فِتْنَةِ المَحْيا وَالمَمـات، وَمِنْ شَرِّ فِتْنَةِ المَسيحِ الدَّجّال .

Allahumma innee aAAoothu bika min AAathabil-qabr, wamin AAathabi jahannam, wamin fitnatil-mahya walmamat, wamin shari fitnatil-maseehid-dajjal.

31

'O Allah, I take refuge in You from the punishment of the grave, from the torment of the Fire, from the trials and tribulations of life and death and from the evil affliction of Al-Maseeh Ad-Dajjal.'

-**Al-Maseeh Ad-Dajjal:** among the great signs of the last hour and the greatest trials to befall mankind, which every Prophet has warned about. Most of mankind will follow him. He will appear from Asbahan, Iran at the time when the Muslims will conquer Constantinople. He will be given special powers and will make the truth seem false and vice versa. He will claim to be righteous and then he will claim prophethood and finally, divinity. From his features is that he will be blind in his right eye which is a definite proof that contradicts his claim to be Allah as it is a sign of imperfection. The word *Kafir* will be written between his eyes which every believer, literate or illiterate will recognise.

(56)

اللّٰهُمَّ إِنِّي أَعُوذُ بِكَ مِنْ عَذَابِ القَبْرِ ، وَأَعُوذُ بِكَ مِنْ فِتْنَةِ المَسِيحِ الدَّجَّالِ ، وَأَعُوذُ بِكَ مِنْ فِتْنَةِ المَحْيَا وَالمَمَاتِ . اللّٰهُمَّ إِنِّي أَعُوذُ بِكَ مِنَ المَأْثَمِ وَالمَغْرَمِ .

Allahumma innee aAAoothu bika min AAathabil-qabr, wa-aAAoothu bika min fitnatil-maseehid-dajjal, wa-aAAoothu bika min fitnatil-mahya walmamat. Allahumma innee aAAoothu bika minal-ma/thami walmaghram.

'O Allah, I take refuge in You from the punishment of the grave, and I take refuge in You from the temptation and trial of Al-Masee<u>h</u> Ad-Dajj<u>al</u>, and I take refuge in You from the trials and tribulations of life and death. O All<u>a</u>h, I take refuge in You from sin and debt.'

(57)

اللّهُـمَّ إِنِّي ظَلَمْتُ نَفْسِي ظُلْمـاً كَثيراً وَلا يَغْـفِرُ الذُّنـوبَ إلاّ أَنْت ، فَاغْـفِر لي مَغْـفِرَةً مِنْ عِنْـدِكَ وَارْحَمْني، إِنَّكَ أَنْتَ الغَفورُ الرَّحـيم .

Allahumma innee _th_alamtu nafsee _th_ulman katheeran wala yaghfiru<u>th</u>-<u>th</u>unooba illa ant, faghfir lee maghfiratan min AAindik war<u>h</u>amnee, innaka antal-Ghafoorur-Ra<u>h</u>eem.

'O All<u>a</u>h, I have indeed oppressed my soul excessively and none can forgive sin except You, so forgive me a forgiveness from Yourself and have mercy upon me. Surely, You are The Most-Forgiving, The Most-Merciful.'

-From Yourself: i.e. from Your innermost grace without deserving it and a forgiveness which is befitting to your tremendous generosity.

(58)

اللّهُـمَّ اغْـفِرْ لي ما قَدَّمْتُ وَما أَخَّرْت ، وَما أَسْـرَرْتُ وَما أَعْلَنْت ، وَما أَسْـرَفْت ، وَما أَنْتَ أَعْلَمُ بِهِ مِنِّي . أَنْتَ المُقَـدِّمُ، وَأَنْتَ المُؤَخِّـرُ لا إِلهَ إلاّ أَنْت .

All<u>a</u>hummagh-fir lee m<u>a</u> qaddamtu, wam<u>a</u> akhkhart, wam<u>a</u> asrartu wam<u>a</u> aAAlant, wam<u>a</u>

asraftt, wama anta aAAlamu bihi minnee, antal-muqaddimu wa-antal-mu-akhkhiru la ilaha illa ant.

'O Allah, forgive me for those sins which have come to pass as well as those which shall come to pass, and those I have committed in secret as well as those I have made public, and where I have exceeded all bounds as well as those things about which You are more knowledgeable. You are *Al-Muqaddim* and *Al-Mu-akhkhir*. None has the right to be worshipped except You.'

-Meaning of *Al-Muqaddim* and *Al-Mu-akhkhir*: Allah puts forward and favours whom He wills from amongst His creation just as He defers and holds back whom He wills in accordance to His wisdom. E.g. Favouring man over the rest of creation, favouring the Prophets over the rest of mankind, favouring Muhammad ﷺ over all the Prophets and Messengers...etc.

(59)

اللّهُمَّ أَعِنِّي عَلى ذِكْرِكَ وَشُكْرِكَ ، وَحُسْنِ عِبادَتِكَ .

Allahumma aAAinnee AAala thikrik, washukrik, wahusni AAibadatik.

'O Allah, help me to remember You, to thank You, and to worship You in the best of manners.'

(60)

اللَّهُمَّ إِنِّي أَعوذُ بِكَ مِنَ البُخْـلِ، وَأَعوذُ بِكَ مِنَ الجُبْنِ، وَأَعوذُ بِكَ مِنْ أَنْ أُرَدَّ إِلى أَرْذَلِ العُمُرِ، وَأَعوذُ بِكَ مِنْ فِتْنَةِ الدُّنْيا وَعَذابِ القَبْرِ .

Allahumma innee aAAoothu bika minal-bukhl, wa-aAAoothu bika minal-jubn, wa-aAAoothu bika min an oradda ila arthalil- AAumur, wa-aAAoothu bika min fitnatid-dunya waAAathabil-qabr.

'O Allah, I take refuge in You from miserliness and cowardice, I take refuge in You lest I be returned to the worst of lives "i.e. old age, being weak, incapable and in a state of fear", and I take refuge in You from the trials and tribulations of this life and the punishment of the grave.'

(61)

اللَّهُمَّ إِنِّي أَسْأَلُكَ الجَنَّةَ وأَعوذُ بِكَ مِنَ النَّارِ .

Allahumma innee as-alukal-jannah, wa-aAAoothu bika minan-nar.

'O Allah, I ask You to grant me Paradise and I take refuge in You from the Fire.'

(62)

اللَّهُمَّ بِعِلْمِكَ الغَيْبَ وَقُدْرَتِكَ عَلى الخَلْقِ أَحْيِني ما عَلِمْتَ الحياةَ خَيْراً لي، وَتَوَفَّني إِذا عَلِمْتَ الوَفاةَ خَيْراً لي، اللَّهُمَّ إِنِّي أَسْأَلُكَ خَشْيَتَكَ في الغَيْبِ وَالشَّهادَةِ، وَأَسْأَلُكَ كَلِمَةَ الحَقِّ في الرِّضا وَالغَضَبِ، وَأَسْأَلُكَ القَصْدَ في الغِنى وَالفَقْرِ،

وَأَسْأَلُكَ نَعِيماً لا يَنْفَد، وَأَسْأَلُكَ قُرَّةَ عَيْنٍ لا تَنْقَطِعُ وَأَسْأَلُكَ الرِّضا بَعْدَ القَضاء، وَأَسْأَلُكَ بَرْدَ الْعَيْشِ بَعْدَ الْمَوْت، وَأَسْأَلُكَ لَذَّةَ النَّظَرِ إلى وَجْهِكَ وَالشَّوْقَ إلى لِقائِك، في غَيرِ ضَرّاءَ مُضِرَّة، وَلا فِتْنَةٍ مُضِلَّة، اللّهُمَّ زَيِّنّا بِزينَةِ الإِيمان، وَاجْعَلنا هُداةً مُهْتَدين .

Allahumma biAAilmikal-ghayb, waqudratika AAalal-khalq, ahyinee ma AAalimtal-hayata khayran lee watawaffanee itha AAalimtal-wafata khayran lee, allahumma innee as-aluka khashyataka fil-ghaybi washshahadah, wa-as-aluka kalimatal-haqqi fir-rida walghadab, wa-as-alukal-qasda fil-ghina walfaqr, wa-as-aluka naAAeeman la yanfad, wa-as-aluka qurrata AAaynin la tanqatiAA, wa-as-alukar-rida baAAdal-qada/, wa-as-aluka bardal-AAayshi baAAdal-mawt, wa-as-aluka laththatan-nathari ila wajhik, washshawqa ila liqa-ik fee ghayri darraa mudirrah, wala fitnatin mudillah, allahumma zayyinna bizeenatil-eeman wajAAalna hudatan muhtadeen.

'O Allah, by Your knowledge of the unseen and Your power over creation, keep me alive so long as You know such life to be good for me and take me if You know death to be better for me. O Allah, make me fearful of You whether in secret or in public and I ask You to make me true in speech, in times of pleasure and anger. I ask you to make me moderate in times of wealth and poverty and I ask You for everlasting bliss and joy which will never cease. I ask You to make me pleased with what You have decreed and for an easy life after death. I ask You for the sweetness of looking upon Your Face and a longing to encounter You in a manner which does not entail a calamity which will bring about harm nor a trial which will cause deviation. O All<u>a</u>h, beautify us with the adornment of faith and make us of those who guide and are rightly guided.'

(63)

اللّهُمَّ إِنِّي أَسْأَلُكَ يا اللهُ بِأَنَّكَ الواحِدُ الأَحَد ،الصَّمَدُ الَّذي لَمْ يَلِدْ وَلَمْ يولَدْ، وَلَمْ يَكنْ لَهُ كُفُواً أَحَد ، أَنْ تَغْفِرْ لي ذُنوبي إِنَّكَ أَنْتَ الغَفورُ الرَّحِّيم .

All<u>a</u>humma innee as-aluka y<u>a</u> All<u>a</u>h bi-annakal-w<u>a</u>hidul-a<u>h</u>adu<u>s</u>-<u>s</u>amad, alla<u>th</u>ee lam yalid walam yoolad, walam yakun lahu kufuwan a<u>h</u>ad, an taghfira lee <u>th</u>unoobee innaka antal-Ghafoorur-Ra<u>h</u>eem.

'O All<u>a</u>h, I ask You O All<u>a</u>h, as You are The One, The Only, *A<u>S</u>-<u>S</u>amad*, The One who begets not, nor was He begotten and there is none like unto Him that You forgive me my sins for verily You are The Oft-Forgiving, Most-Merciful.'

-A<u>S</u>-<u>S</u>amad: The Self-Sufficient Master, Possessor of perfect attributes whom all of creation turn to in all their needs.

اللّٰهُمَّ إِنِّي أَسْأَلُكَ بِأَنَّ لَكَ الْحَمْدُ لا إِلهَ إِلاَّ أَنْتَ وَحْدَكَ لا شَرِيكَ لَكَ الْمَنَّانُ يا بَدِيعَ السَّمواتِ وَالأَرْضِ يا ذا الْجَلالِ وَالإِكْرام، يا حَيُّ يا قَيّومُ إِنِّي أَسْأَلُكَ الْجَنَّةَ وَأَعوذُ بِكَ مِنَ النَّار .

Allahumma innee as-aluka bianna lakal-hamd, la ilaha illa ant wahdaka la shareeka lak, almannan, ya badeeAAas-samawati wal-ard, ya thal-jalali wal-ikram, ya hayyu ya qayyoom, innee as-alukal-jannah, wa-aAAoothu bika minan-nar.

'O Allah, I ask You as unto You is all praise, none has the right to be worshipped except You, alone, without partner. You are the Benefactor. O Originator of the heavens and the Earth, O Possessor of majesty and honour, O Ever Living, O Self-Subsisting and Supporter of all, verily I ask You for Paradise and I take refuge with You from the Fire.'

اللّٰهُمَّ إِنِّي أَسْأَلُكَ بِأَنِّي أَشْهَدُ أَنَّكَ أَنْتَ اللهُ لا إِلهَ إِلاَّ أَنْت ، الأَحَدُ الصَّمَدُ الَّذي لَمْ يَلِدْ وَلَمْ يولَدْ ، وَلَمْ يَكُنْ لَهُ كُفُواً أَحَـد .

Allahumma inne as-aluka biannee ashhadu annaka antal-lah, la ilaha illa ant, al-ahadus-samad, allathee lam yalid walam yoolad walam yakun lahu kufuwan ahad.

'O All<u>a</u>h, I ask You, as I bear witness that You are
All<u>a</u>h, none has the right to be worshipped except
You, The One, *A<u>S</u>-<u>S</u>amad* Who begets not nor was He
begotten and there is none like unto Him.'

-A<u>S</u>-<u>S</u>amad: The Self-Sufficient Master, Possessor of
perfect attributes whom all of creation turn to in all
their needs.

25. REMEMBRANCE AFTER SAL<u>A</u>M

(66)

أَسْتَغْفِرُ اللهَ . (ثَلاثاً)

اللَّهُمَّ أَنْتَ السَّلامُ ، وَمِنْكَ السَّلامُ ، تَبَارَكْتَ يا ذا الجَلالِ
وَالإِكْرامِ .

Astaghfirul-l<u>a</u>h (three times)
**All<u>a</u>humma   antas-sal<u>a</u>m   waminkas-sal<u>a</u>m,
tab<u>a</u>rakta ya <u>th</u>al-jal<u>a</u>li wal-ikr<u>a</u>m.**

'I ask All<u>a</u>h for forgiveness.' (three times)
'O All<u>a</u>h, You are *As-Sal<u>a</u>m* and from You is all peace,
blessed are You, O Possessor of majesty and honour.'

-AS-Sal<u>a</u>m: The One Who is free from all defects and
deficiencies.

(67)

لا إلهَ إلاّ اللّهُ وحدَهُ لا شريكَ لهُ، لهُ المُلْكُ ولهُ الحَمْد، وهوَ
على كلّ شَيءٍ قَدير، اللّهُمَّ لا مانِعَ لِما أَعْطَيْت، وَلا مُعْطِيَ لِما
مَنَعْت، وَلا يَنْفَعُ ذا الجَدِّ مِنْكَ الجَد .

La ilaha illal-lahu wahdahu la shareeka lah, lahul-mulku walahul-hamd, wahuwa AAala kulli shayin qadeer, allahumma la maniAAa lima aAAtayt, wala muAAtiya lima manaAAt, wala yanfaAAu thal-jaddi minkal-jad.

'None has the right to be worshipped except Allah, alone, without partner, to Him belongs all sovereignty and praise and He is over all things omnipotent.O Allah, none can prevent what You have willed to bestow and none can bestow what You have willed to prevent, and no wealth or majesty can benefit anyone, as from You is all wealth and majesty.'

(68)

لا إلهَ إلاّ اللّه, وحدَهُ لا شريكَ لهُ، لهُ المُلكُ ولهُ الحَمد، وهوَ على كلّ شيءٍ قدير، لا حَوْلَ وَلا قـوّةَ إلاّ بِاللّهِ، لا إلهَ إلاّ اللّه، وَلا نَعْبُدُ إلاّ إيّاه, لَهُ النّعْمَةُ وَلَهُ الفَضْل وَلَهُ الثّناءُ الحَسَن، لا إلهَ إلاّ اللّهُ مُخْلِصينَ لَهُ الدّينَ وَلَوْ كَرِهَ الكافِرون .

La ilaha illal-lah, wahdahu la shareeka lah, lahul-mulku walahul-hamd, wahuwa AAala kulli shayin qadeer. la hawla wala quwwata illa billah, la ilaha illal-lah, wala naAAbudu illa iyyah, lahun-niAAmatu walahul-fadl walahuth-thana-ol- hasan, la ilaha illal-lah mukhliseena lahud-deen walaw karihal-kafiroon.

'None has the right to be worshipped except Allah, alone, without partner, to Him belongs all sovereignty and praise and He is over all things omnipotent. There is no might nor power except with All<u>a</u>h, none has the right to be worshipped except All<u>a</u>h and we worship none except Him. For Him is all favour, grace, and glorious praise. None has the right to be worshipped except All<u>a</u>h and we are sincere in faith and devotion to Him although the disbelievers detest it.'

(69)

سُبْحانَ اللهِ، والحَمْـدُ لله ، واللهُ أَكْـبَر . (ثلاثاً وثلاثين)

لا إلهَ إلاَّ اللّهُ وَحْـدَهُ لا شريكَ لهُ، لهُ الملكُ ولهُ الحَمْد، وهُوَ

على كُلّ شيءٍ قَـدير .

Subh<u>a</u>nal-l<u>a</u>h walhamdu lill<u>a</u>h, wall<u>a</u>hu akbar (thirty-three times).

L<u>a</u> il<u>a</u>ha illal-l<u>a</u>hu wa<u>h</u>dahu l<u>a</u> shareeka lah, lahul-mulku walahul-<u>h</u>amd, wahuwa AAal<u>a</u> kulli shayin qadeer.

'How perfect All<u>a</u>h is, all praise is for All<u>a</u>h, and All<u>a</u>h is the greatest.' (thirty-three times)

'None has the right to be worshipped except All<u>a</u>h, alone, without partner, to Him belongs all sovereignty and praise and He is over all things omnipotent.'

(70)

The following three chapters should be recited once after <u>Th</u>uhr, AAa<u>s</u>r and AAisha prayers and thrice after Fajr and Maghrib.

﴿ قُلْ هُوَ اللّهُ أَحَـدٌ .....﴾ [الإِخْـلاصْ]

{Qul huwa All<u>a</u>hu a<u>h</u>ad...} [Al-Ikhl<u>a</u>s]

41

﴿ قُلْ أَعُوذُ بِرَبِّ الفَلَقِ.....﴾ [الفَلَقْ]

{Qul aAAoo<u>th</u>u birabbi alfalaq.....} [Al-Falaq]

﴿ قُلْ أَعُوذُ بِرَبِّ النَّاسِ.....﴾ [النَّاس]

{Qul aAAoo<u>th</u>u birabbi alnn<u>a</u>s.....} [An-N<u>a</u>s]

(71)

It is also from the sunnah to recite the verse of the Footstool (<u>A</u>yat-Al-Kursiy) after each prayer:

﴿ اللَّهُ لا إِلَهَ إِلاَّ هُوَ الْحَيُّ القَيُّومُ لا تَأْخُذُهُ سِنَةٌ وَلا نَوْمٌ
..... ﴾

{All<u>a</u>hu l<u>a</u> il<u>a</u>ha ill<u>a</u> huwa al<u>h</u>ayyu alqayyoomu l<u>a</u> ta/khu<u>th</u>uhu sinatun wal<u>a</u> nawm...}
[Al-Baqarah:255]

(72)

لا إِلَهَ إِلاَّ اللَّهُ وَحْدَهُ لا شَرِيكَ لَهُ، لَهُ الْمُلْكُ ولهُ الْحَمْد، يُحْيِي
وَيُمِيتُ وهُوَ على كُلِّ شيءٍ قدير . (عَشْر مَرَّات بَعْدَ المَغْرِب
وَالصّبْح)

L<u>a</u> il<u>a</u>ha illal-l<u>a</u>hu wa<u>h</u>dahu l<u>a</u> shareeka lah, lahul-mulku walahul-<u>h</u>amd, yu<u>h</u>yee wayumeet, wahuwa AAal<u>a</u> kulli shayin qadeer. (ten times after the maghrib & fajr prayers)

'None has the right to be worshipped except All<u>a</u>h, alone, without partner, to Him belongs all sovereignty and praise, He gives life and causes death and He is over all things omnipotent.'
(ten times after the maghrib and fajr prayers)

---

(73)

اللّهُـمَّ إِنِّي أَسْأَلُكَ عِلْماً نافِعاً وَرِزْقاً طَيِّباً ، وَعَمَلاً مُتَقَبَّلاً .

(بَعْد السَّلام من صَلاةِ الفَجْرِ)

Allahumma innee as-aluka AAilman nafiAAan, warizqan tayyiban, waAAamalan mutaqabbalan.
(after salam from fajr prayer)

'O Allah, I ask You for knowledge which is beneficial and sustenance which is good, and deeds which are acceptable.' (To be said after giving salam for the fajr prayer)

---

26. SUPPLICATION FOR SEEKING GUIDANCE IN FORMING A DECISION OR CHOOSING THE PROPER COURSE...ETC (AL-ISTIKHARAH)

(74)

On the authority of Jabir Ibn AAabdullah ﷺ, he said: ' The Prophet ﷺ would instruct us to pray for guidance in all of our concerns, just as he would teach us a chapter from the Quran. He ﷺ would say ' If any of you intends to undertake a matter then let him pray two supererogatory units (two rakAAah nafilah) of prayer and after which he should supplicate:

اللّهُـمَّ إِنِّي أَسْتَخِيرُكَ بِعِلْمِكَ، وَأَسْتَقْدِرُكَ بِقُدْرَتِكَ، وَأَسْأَلُكَ مِنْ فَضْلِكَ العَظِيمِ، فَإِنَّكَ تَقْدِرُ وَلا أَقْدِرِ، وَتَعْلَمُ وَلا أَعْلَمَ، وَأَنْتَ عَلّامُ الغُيوبِ، اللّهُـمَّ إِنْ كُنْتَ تَعْلَمُ أَنَّ هـذا الأَمْرَ- وَيُسَمِّي حاجَتَه - خَيْرٌ لي في ديني وَمَعاشي وَعاقِبَةِ أَمْري، فَاقْدُرْهُ لي وَيَسِّرْهُ لي ثـمَّ بارِكْ لي فيهِ، وَإِنْ كُنْتَ تَعْلَمُ

أَنَّ هـذا الأَمْـرَ شَـرٌّ لي في دينـي وَمَعـاشي وَعاقِبَةِ أَمْري، فَاصْرِفْهُ وَاصْرِفْني عَنْـهُ وَاقْدُرْ لي الخَيْرَ حَيْثُ كانَ ثُمَّ أَرْضِنـي بِـه .

Allahumma innee astakheeruka biAAilmik, wa-astaqdiruka biqudratik, wa-as-aluka min fadlikal-AAatheem, fa-innaka taqdiru wala aqdir, wataAAlamu wala aAAlam ,wa-anta AAallamul ghuyoob, allahumma in kunta taAAlamu anna hathal-amr (say your need) **khayrun lee fee deenee wamaAAashee waAAaqibati amree faqdurhu lee, wayassirhu lee, thumma barik lee feeh, wa-in kunta taAAlamu anna hathal-amr sharrun lee fee deenee wamaAAashee waAAaqibati amree fasrifhu AAannee wasrifnee AAanh, waqdur liyal-khayra haythu kan, thumma ardinee bih.**

'O Allah, I seek Your counsel by Your knowledge and by Your power I seek strength and I ask You from Your immense favour, for verily You are able while I am not and verily You know while I do not and You are the Knower of the unseen. O Allah, if You know this affair -*and here he mentions his need*- to be good for me in relation to my religion, my life, and end, then decree and facilitate it for me, and bless me with it, and if You know this affair to be ill for me towards my religion, my life, and end, then remove it from me and remove me from it, and decree for me what is good wherever it be and make me satisfied with such.'

One who seeks guidance from his Creator and consults his fellow believers and then remains firm in his resolve does not regret, for Allah has said:

﴿ وَشَاوِرْهُم فِي الأَمْرِ فَإِذا عَزَمْتَ فَتَوَكَّـلْ عَلَى الله ﴾

⟨washawirhum fee al-amri fa-itha AAazamta fatawakkal AAala Allah ⟩

(chapter 3 verse 159)

'…and consult them in the affair. Then when you have taken a decision, put your trust in Allah…'

27. REMEMBRANCE SAID IN THE MORNING AND EVENING

-(as-sabah) translated *morning*: after Fajr prayer until the sun rises, (al-masa/) translated *evening*: after AAsr prayer until the sunsets, however some scholars say: after the sunsets and onwards.

(75)

In the evening:

أَمْسَيْنا وَأَمْسى المُلكُ لله وَالحَمدُ لله ، لا إلهَ إلاّ اللّهُ وَحدَهُ لا شَريكَ لهُ، لهُ المُـلكُ ولهُ الحَمْـد، وهُوَ على كلّ شَيءٍ قديرٍ ، رَبِّ أَسْأَلُكَ خَـيرَ ما في هـذهِ اللَّيْلةِ وَخَـيرَ ما بَعْدَها ، وَأَعوذُ بِكَ مِنْ شَرِّ هـذهِ اللَّيْلةِ وَشَرِّ ما بَعْدَها ، رَبِّ أَعوذُبِكَ مِنَ الْكَسَلِ وَسوءِ الْكِبَرِ ، رَبِّ أَعوذُبِكَ مِنْ عَذابٍ في النّارِ وَعَذابٍ في القَبْرِ .

Amsayna wa-amsal-mulku lillah walhamdu lillah la ilaha illal-lah, wahdahu la shareeka lah, lahul-

mulku walahul-ḥamd, wahuwa AAalā kulli shayin qadeer, rabbi as-aluka khayra mā fee hathihil-laylah, wakhayra mā baAAdahā, wa-aAAoothu bika min sharri hathihil-laylah, washarri mā baAAdahā, rabbi aAAoothu bika minal-kasal, wasoo-il kibar, rabbi aAAoothu bika min AAathabin fin-nar, waAAathabin fil-qabr.

'We have reached the evening and at this very time unto Allāh belongs all sovereignty, and all praise is for Allāh.   None has the right to be worshipped except Allāh, alone, without partner, to Him belongs all sovereignty and praise and He is over all things omnipotent. My Lord, I ask You for the good of this night and the good of what follows it and I take refuge in You from the evil of this night and the evil of what follows it.   My Lord, I take refuge in You from laziness and senility. My Lord, I take refuge in You from torment in the Fire and punishment in the grave.'

…likewise, one says in the morning:

أَصْبَحْنا وَأَصْبَحَ المُلْكُ لله ......

Asbahna wa-asbahal-mulku lillāh...

'We have reached the morning and at this very time unto Allāh belongs all sovereignty…'

(76)

اللّهُمَّ بِكَ أَصْبَحْنا وَبِكَ أَمْسَيْنا ، وَبِكَ نَحْيا وَبِكَ نَموتُ وَإِلَيْكَ النُّشور .

Allāhumma bika asbahna wabika amsaynā, wabika nahya ,wabika namootu wa-ilaykan-nushoor.

'O Allah, by your leave we have reached the morning and by Your leave we have reached the evening, by Your leave we live and die and unto You is our resurrection.'

In the evening:

اللّهُمَّ بِكَ أَمْسَينا، وَبِكَ أَصْبَحْنا، وَبِكَ نَحْيا، وَبِكَ نَموتُ وَإِلَيْكَ المَصير.

Alla̲humma bika amsayna̲, wabika asbahna̲, wabika nahya wabika namootu wa-ilaykal-maseer.

'O Alla̲h, by Your leave we have reached the evening and by Your leave we have reached the morning, by Your leave we live and die and unto You is our return.'

(77)

اللّهمَّ أَنْتَ رَبِّي لا إلهَ إلاَّ أَنْتَ ، خَلَقْتَني وَأَنا عَبْدُك ، وَأَنا عَلى عَهْدِكَ وَوَعْدِكَ ما اسْتَطَعْت ، أَعوذُبِكَ مِنْ شَرِّ ما صَنَعْت ، أَبوءُ لَكَ بِنِعْمَتِكَ عَلَيَّ وَأَبوءُ بِذَنْبي فَاغْفِرْ لي فَإِنَّهُ لا يَغْفِرُ الذُّنوبَ إلاَّ أَنْتَ .

Alla̲humma anta rabbee la̲ ila̲ha illa̲ ant, khalaqtanee wa-ana̲ AAabduk, wa-ana̲ AAala̲ AAahdika wawaAAdika mas-tataAAt, aAAoothu bika min sharri ma̲ sanaAAt, aboo-o laka biniAAmatika AAalay, wa-aboo-o bithanbee, faghfir lee fa-innahu la̲ yaghfiruth-thunooba illa̲ ant.

'O Allah, You are my Lord, none has the right to be worshipped except You, You created me and I am Your servant and I abide to Your covenant and promise as best I can, I take refuge in You from the evil of which I have committed. I acknowledge Your favour upon me and I acknowledge my sin, so forgive me, for verily none can forgive sin except You.'

(78)

اللّهُمَّ إِنِّي أَصْبَحْتُ أُشْهِدُك ، وَأُشْهِدُ حَمَلَةَ عَرْشِك ، وَمَلائِكَتِك ، وَجَمِيعَ خَلْقِك ، أَنَّكَ أَنْتَ اللهُ لا إلهَ إِلاَّ أَنْتَ وَحْدَكَ لا شَرِيكَ لَك ، وَأَنَّ مُحَمّداً عَبْدُكَ وَرَسولُك. (أربع مرات حينَ يصْبِح أوْ يمسي)

Allahumma innee asbahtu oshhiduk, wa-oshhidu hamalata AAarshik, wamala-ikatak, wajameeAAa khalqik, annaka antal-lahu la ilaha illa ant, wahdaka la shareeka lak, wa-anna Muhammadan AAabduka warasooluk (four times in the morning & evening).

'O Allah, verily I have reached the morning and call on You, the bearers of Your throne, Your angles, and all of Your creation to witness that You are Allah, none has the right to be worshipped except You, alone, without partner and that Muhammad is Your Servant and Messenger.' (four times in the morning and evening.)

-Note: for the evening, one reads (amsaytu) instead of (asbahtu).

اللّهُمَّ ما أَصْبَحَ بي مِنْ نِعْمَةٍ أَو بِأَحَدٍ مِنْ خَلْقِكَ ، فَمِنْكَ وَحْدَكَ لا شريكَ لَكَ ، فَلَكَ الْحَمْدُ وَلَكَ الشُّكر .

Allahumma ma asbaha bee min niAAmatin, aw bi-ahadin min khalqik, faminka wahdaka la shareeka lak, falakal-hamdu walakash-shukr.

'O Allah, what blessing I or any of Your creation have risen upon, is from You alone, without partner, so for You is all praise and unto You all thanks.'

…whoever says this in the morning has indeed offered his day's thanks and whoever says this in the evening has indeed offered his night's thanks.

-Note: for the evening, one reads (amsa) instead of (asbaha).

اللّهُمَّ عافِني في بَدَني ، اللّهُمَّ عافِني في سَمْعي ، اللّهُمَّ عافِني في بَصَري ، لا إلهَ إلاّ اللهُ أَنْتَ. (ثلاثاً)

اللّهُمَّ إنّي أَعوذُبِكَ مِنَ الْكُفر ، وَالفَقْر ، وَأَعوذُبِكَ مِنْ عَذابِ القَبْر ، لا إلهَ إلاّ أَنْتَ . (ثلاثاً)

Allahumma AAafinee fee badanee, allahumma AAafinee fee samAAee, allahumma AAafinee fee basaree, la ilaha illa ant. (three times)

Allahumma innee aAAoothu bika minal-kufr, walfaqr, wa-aAAoothu bika min AAathabil-qabr, la ilaha illa ant. (three times)

'O Allah, grant my body health, O Allah, grant my hearing health, O Allah, grant my sight health. None has the right to be worshipped except You.' (three times)

'O All<u>a</u>h, I take refuge with You from disbelief and poverty, and I take refuge with You from the punishment of the grave. None has the right to be worshipped except You.' (three times)

(81)

حَسْبِيَ اللّهُ لا إلَهَ إلاَّ هُوَ عَلَيهِ تَوَكَّلتُ وَهُوَ رَبُّ العَرْشِ العَظيم . (سبع مَرّات حينَ يصْبِح وَيمسي)

Hasbiyal-l<u>a</u>hu la il<u>a</u>ha ill<u>a</u> huwa, AAalayhi tawakkalt, wahuwa rabbul-AAarshil-Aaa*th*eem. (seven times morning & evening)

'All<u>a</u>h is Sufficient for me, none has the right to be worshipped except Him, upon Him I rely and He is Lord of the exalted throne.' (seven times morning and evening)

(82)

أَعوذُبِكَلِمـاتِ اللّهِ التّامَاتِ مِنْ شَرِّ ما خَلَق . (ثلاثاً إذا أمسى)

aAAoo*th*u bikalimatil-l<u>a</u>hit-t<u>a</u>mm<u>a</u>ti min sharri ma khalaq. (three times in the evening)

'I take refuge in All<u>a</u>h's perfect words from the evil He has created.' (three times in the evening).

(83)

اللّهُمَّ إِنّي أَسْأَلُكَ العَفْوَ والعـافِيةَ في الدُّنْيا والآخِرَة ، اللّهُمَّ إِنّي أَسْأَلُكَ العَفْوَ والعـافِيةَ في ديني وَدُنْـيايَ وَأَهْلي وَمالي ،

اللّهُمَّ اسْتُرْ عَوْراتِي وَآمِنْ رَوْعاتِي ، اللّهُمَّ احْفَظْنِي مِن بَيْنِ يَدَيَّ وَمِن خَلْفِي وَعَن يَمِينِي وَعَن شِمالِي ، وَمِن فَوْقِي ، وَأَعوذُ بِعَظَمَتِكَ أَن أُغْتالَ مِن تَحْتِي .

Allahumma innee as-alukal-AAafwa walAAafiyah, fid-dunya wal-akhirah, allahumma innee as-alukal-AAafwa walAAafiyah fee deenee, wadunyaya wa-ahlee, wamalee, allahummas-tur AAawratee, wa-amin rawAAatee, allahummah-fathnee min bayni yaday, wamin khalfee, waAAan yameenee, waAAan shimalee, wamin fawqee, wa-aAAoothu biAAathamatika an oghtala min tahtee.

'O Allah, I ask You for pardon and well-being in this life and the next. O Allah, I ask You for pardon and well-being in my religious and worldly affairs, and my family and my wealth. O Allah, veil my weaknesses and set at ease my dismay. O Allah, preserve me from the front and from behind and on my right and on my left and from above, and I take refuge with You lest I be swallowed up by the earth.'

(84)

اللّهُمَّ عالِمَ الغَيْبِ وَالشَّهادَةِ فاطِرَ السّماواتِ وَالأرْضِ رَبَّ كُلِّ شَيءٍ وَمَلِيكَه ، أَشْهَدُ أَنْ لا إِلهَ إِلاّ أَنْت ، أَعوذُ بِكَ مِن شَرِّ نَفْسِي وَمِن شَرِّ الشَّيْطانِ وَشِرْكِه ، وَأَنْ أَقْتَرِفَ عَلى نَفْسِي سوءاً أَوْ أَجُرَّهُ إِلى مُسْلِم .

Allahumma AAalimal-ghaybi washshahadah, fatiras-samawati wal-ard, rabba kulli shayin wamaleekah, ashhadu an la ilaha illa ant, aAAoothu bika min sharri nafsee wamin sharrish-shaytani washirkih, waan aqtarifa AAala nafsee soo-an aw ajurrahu ila muslim.

'O Allah, Knower of the unseen and the seen, Creator of the heavens and the Earth, Lord and Sovereign of all things, I bear witness that none has the right to be worshipped except You. I take refuge in You from the evil of my soul and from the evil and *shirk* of the devil, and from committing wrong against my soul or bringing such upon another Muslim.'

-*shirk*: to associate others with Allah in those things which are specific to Him. This can occur in (1) belief, e.g. to believe that other than Allah has the power to benefit or harm, (2) speech, e.g. to swear by other than Allah and (3) action, e.g. to bow or prostrate to other than Allah.

(85)

بِسِمِ اللهِ الذي لا يَضُرُّ مَعَ اسمِهِ شَيءٌ في الأُرْضِ وَلا في السّماءِ وَهـوَ السّمـيـعُ العَلـيـم . (ثلاثاً)

Bismil-lahil-lathee la yadurru maAAas-mihi shay-on fil-ardi wala fis-sama-i wahuwas-sameeAAul-AAaleem. (three times)

'In the name of Allah with whose name nothing is harmed on earth nor in the heavens and He is The All-Seeing, The All-Knowing.' (three times)

(86)

رَضيتُ بِاللهِ رَبّاً وَبِالإِسْلامِ ديناً وَبِمُحَمَّدٍ ﷺ نَبِيّاً . (ثلاثاً)

Radeetu billahi rabban wabil-islami deenan wabiMuhammadin ﷺ nabiyya. (three times)

'I am pleased with Allah as a Lord, and Islam as a religion and Muhammad ﷺ as a Prophet.' (three times)

(87)

سُبْحـانَ اللهِ وَبِحَمْـدِهِ عَدَدَ خَلْقِه ، وَرِضـا نَفْسِـه ، وَزِنَـةَ عَـرْشِـه ، وَمِـدادَ كَلِمـاتِه . (ثلاثاً)

Subhanal-lahi wabihamdih, AAadada khalqihi warida nafsih, wazinata AAarshih, wamidada kalimatih. (three times)

'How perfect Allah is and I praise Him by the number of His creation and His pleasure, and by the weight of His throne, and the ink of His words.' (three times)

(88)

سُبْحـانَ اللهِ وَبِحَمْـدِهِ . (مائة مرة)

Subhanal-lahi wabihamdih. (one hundred times)

'How perfect Allah is and I praise Him.' (one hundred times)

(89)

يا حَيُّ يا قَيّومُ بِرَحْمَتِكِ أَسْتَغيـث ، أَصْلِحْ لي شَـأْني كُلَّه ، وَلا تَكِلْني إلى نَفْسي طَرْفَةَ عَين .

Ya hayyu ya qayyoom, birahmatika astagheeth, aslih lee sha/nee kullah, wala takilnee ila nafsee tarfata AAayn.

'O Ever Living, O Self-Subsisting and Supporter of all, by Your mercy I seek assistance, rectify for me all of my affairs and do not leave me to myself, even for the blink of an eye.'

(90)

لا إلهَ إلاَّ اللّهُ وحْدَهُ لا شَرِيكَ لهُ، لهُ المُلْكُ ولهُ الحَمْـد، وهُوَ

على كُلّ شَيءٍ قَدِير . (مائة مرة)

La ilaha illal-lah, wahdahu la shareeka lah, lahul-mulku walahul-hamd, wahuwa AAala kulli shay-in qadeer. (one hundred times)

'None has the right to be worshipped except Allah, alone, without partner, to Him belongs all sovereignty and praise, and He is over all things omnipotent.' (one hundred times every day)

(91)

أَصْبَحْنا وَأَصْبَحْ المُلكُ للهِ رَبِّ العالَمِين ، اللّهُمَّ إنِّي

أَسْـأَلُكَ خَيْرَ هذا اليَوْم ، فَتْحَهُ ، وَنَصْرَهُ ، وَنـورَهُ وَبَـرَكَتَهُ ،

وَهُداهُ ، وَأَعوذُ بِكَ مِنْ شَرِّ ما فيهِ وَشَرِّ ما بَعْـدَه .

Asbahna wa-asbahal-mulku lillahi rabbil-AAalameen, allahumma innee as-aluka khayra hathal-yawm, fat-hahu, wanasrahu, wanoorahu, wabarakatahu, wahudahu, wa-aAAoothu bika min sharri ma feehi, washarri ma baAAdah.

'We have reached the morning and at this very time all sovereignty belongs to Allah, Lord of the worlds. O Allah, I ask You for the good of this day, its triumphs and its victories, its light and its blessings and its guidance, and I take refuge in You from the evil of this day and the evil that follows it.'

For the evening, the supplication is read as follows:

أَمْسَيْنا وَأَمْسى المُلكُ للهِ رَبِّ العـالَمِين ، اللّهُمَّ إِنِّي أَسْأَلُكَ خَـيْرَ هذهِ اللَّيْلَة ، فَتْحَها ، وَنَصْرَها ، وَنورَها وَبَرَكَتَها ، وَهُداها ، وَأَعوذُ بِكَ مِنْ شَرِّ ما فيها وَشَرِّ ما بَعْدَها .

Amsayna wa-amsal-mulku lillahi rabbil-AAalameen, allahumma innee as-aluka khayra hathihil-laylah, fat-haha, wanasraha, wanooraha, wabarakataha, wahudaha, wa-aAAoothu bika min sharri ma feeha washarri ma baAAdaha.

'We have reached the evening and at this very time all sovereignty belongs to Allah, Lord of the worlds. O Allah, I ask You for the good of tonight, its triumphs and its victories, its light and its blessings and its guidance, and I take refuge in You from the evil of tonight and the evil that follows it.'

(92)

The messenger of Allah ﷺ said: 'Whoever says in the morning:

لا إلهَ إلاَّ اللّهُ وحْـدَهُ لا شَريكَ لهُ، لهُ المُلكُ ولهُ الحَمْد، وهُوَ على كُلّ شَيءٍ قَـدير .

La ilaha illal-lahu wahdahu la shareeka lah, lahul-mulk, walahul-hamd, wahuwa AAala kulli shayin qadeer.

'None has the right to be worshipped except Allah, alone, without partner, to Him belongs all sovereignty and praise and He is over all things omnipotent.'

…has indeed gained the reward of freeing a slave from the children of IsmaAAeel, and ten of his sins are wiped away and he is raised ten degrees, and he has found a safe retreat from the devil until evening. Similarly, if he says it at evening time, he will be protected until the morning.'

(93)

أَصْبَحْنا على فِطْرَةِ الإِسْلام ، وَعَلى كَلِمَةِ الإِخْلاص ، وَعلى دِينِ نَبِيِّنا مُحَمَّدٍ ﷺ وَعَلى مِلَّةِ أبينا إِبْراهِيمَ حَنِيفاً مُسْلِماً وَما كانَ مِنَ المُشْرِكينَ .

Asbahna AAala fitratil-islam, waAAala kalimatil-ikhlas, waAAala deeni nabiyyina Muhammad ﷺ waAAala millati abeena Ibraheem, haneefan musliman wama kana minal-mushrikeen.

'We rise upon the *fitrah* of Islam, and the word of pure faith, and upon the religion of our Prophet Muhammad ﷺ and the religion of our forefather Ibraheem, who was a Muslim and of true faith and was not of those who associate others with Allah.'

-fitrah: the religion of Islam, the way of Ibraheem (pbuh).

-pure faith: the Shahada.

-Note:

في المَساء تُسْتَبْدَل كَلِمَةُ أَصْبَحْنا بِكَلِمَةِ أَمْسَينا.

For the evening, one reads **amsayna** instead of
asbahna.

(94)

'AAabdullah Ibn Khubaib ⬥ said: 'The Messenger of
Allah ﷺ said to me 'Recite!' I replied 'O Messenger of
Allah, what shall I recite?' he said 'Recite:

[الإِخْـلاصْ] ﴿.....أَحَـدٌ اللهُ هُوَ قُلْ ﴾

{Qul huwa Allahu ahad...}   [Al-Ikhlas]

[الفَلَـقْ] ﴿.....الفَلَـقِ بِرَبِّ أَعـوذُ قُلْ ﴾

{Qul aAAoothu birabbi alfalaq.....} [Al-Falaq]

[النّـاسِ] ﴿.....النّـاسِ بِرَبِّ أَعـوذُ قُلْ ﴾

{Qul aAAoothu birabbi alnnas.....} [An-Nas]

...in the evening and the morning three times for it will
suffice you of all else.'

28. REMEMBRANCE BEFORE SLEEPING

(95)

'When retiring to his bed every night, the Prophet ﷺ
would hold his palms together, spit (A form of spitting
comprising mainly of air with little spittle) in them, recite
the last three chapters (Al-Ikhlas, Al-Falaq, An-Nas) of the
Quran and then wipe over his entire body as much as
possible with his hands, beginning with his head and face
and then all parts of the body, he would do this three
times.'

(96)

The Prophet ﷺ also said: 'When you are about to sleep
recite ayat-al-kursee (The verse of the foot-stool, chapter

2:255) till the end of the verse for there will remain over you a protection from Allah and no devil will draw near to you until morning.'

(97)

The Prophet ﷺ also said: 'Whoever recites the last two verses of Soorat Al-Baqarah at night, those two verses shall be sufficient for him (i.e. protect him from all that can cause him harm).'

﴿ آمَنَ الرَّسُولُ بِمَا أُنْزِلَ إِلَيْهِ مِنْ رَبِّهِ وَالْمُؤْمِنُونَ.... ﴾

﴿**Amana alrrasoolu bima onzila ilayhi min rabbihi wa almu/minoona....**﴾

[Al-Baqarah: 285-286]

(98)

'If one of you rises from his bed and then returns to it he should dust it with the edge of his garment three times for he does not know what has occurred in his absence and when he lies down he should supplicate:

بِاسْمِكَ رَبِّي وَضَعْتُ جَنْبِي ، وَبِكَ أَرْفَعُهُ، فَإِنْ أَمْسَكْتَ نَفْسِي فَارْحَمْهَا ، وَإِنْ أَرْسَلْتَهَا فَاحْفَظْهَا بِمَا تَحْفَظُ بِهِ عِبَادَكَ الصَّالِحِينَ .

Bismika rabbee wadaAAtu janbee wabika arfaAAuh, fa-in amsakta nafsee farhamha, wa-in arsaltaha fahfathha bima tahfathu bihi AAibadakas-saliheen.

'In Your name my Lord, I lie down and in Your name I rise, so if You should take my soul then have mercy upon it, and if You should return my soul then protect it in the manner You do so with Your righteous servants.'

(99)

اللّهُمَّ إِنَّكَ خَلَقْتَ نَفْسِي وَأَنْتَ تَوَفَّاها لَكَ مَماتها وَمُحْياها ، إِنْ أَحْيَيْتَها فاحْفَظْها ، وَإِنْ أَمَتَّها فاغْفِرْ لَها . اللّهُمَّ إِنِّي أَسْأَلُكَ العافِيَة .

Allahumma innaka khalaqta nafsee wa-anta tawaffaha, laka mamatuha wamahyaha in ahyaytaha fahfathha, wa-in amattaha faghfir laha. Allahumma innee as-alukal-AAafiyah.

'O Allah, verily You have created my soul and You shall take it's life, to You belongs it's life and death. If You should keep my soul alive then protect it, and if You should take it's life then forgive it. O Allah, I ask You to grant me good health.'

(100)

The Prophet ﷺ would place his right hand under his cheek when about to sleep and supplicate:

اللّهُمَّ قِنِي عَذابَكَ يَوْمَ تَبْعَثُ عِبادَك . (ثلاثاً)

Allahumma qinee AAathabaka yawma tabAAathu AAibadak. (three times).

'O Allah, protect me from Your punishment on the day Your servants are resurrected.' (three times)

(101)

بِاسْمِكَ اللّهُمَّ أَموتُ وَأَحْيا .

Bismikal-lahumma amootu wa-ahya.

'In Your name O All<u>a</u>h, I live and die.'

(102)

'Shall I not direct you both (The Prophet ﷺ was addressing Ali and F<u>a</u>timah-may All<u>a</u>h be pleased with them- when they approached him for a servant) to something better than a servant? When you go to bed say:

سُبْحانَ اللهِ (ثَلاثاً وَثَلاثينَ)

Sub<u>h</u>anal-l<u>a</u>h. (thirty-three times)
'How Perfect All<u>a</u>h is.' (thirty-three times)

الحمدُ لله (ثَلاثاً وَثَلاثينَ)

Al<u>h</u>amdu lill<u>a</u>h. (thirty-three times)
'All praise is for All<u>a</u>h.' (thirty-three times)

اللهُ أَكْبر (أَربعاً وَثَلاثينَ)

All<u>a</u>hu akbar. (thirty-four times)
'All<u>a</u>h is the greatest.' (thirty-four times)
...for that is indeed better for you both than a servant.'

(103)

اللّهُمَّ رَبَّ السَّموَاتِ السَّبْعِ وَرَبَّ العَرْشِ العَظيمِ ، رَبَّنا وَرَبَّ كُلِّ شَيءٍ ، فالِقَ الحَبِّ وَالنَّوى ، وَمُنَزِّلَ التَّوْراةِ وَالإنْجِيلِ ، والفُرْقانِ ، أَعوذُ بِكَ مِن شَرِّ كُلِّ شَيءٍ أَنْتَ آخِذٌ بِناصِيَتِهِ . اللّهُمَّ أَنْتَ الأَوَّلُ فَلَيسَ قَبْلَكَ شَيء ، وَأَنْتَ الآخِرُفَلَيسَ بَعْدَكَ شَيء ، وَأَنْتَ الظّاهِرُ فَلَيْسَ فَوْقَكَ شَيء

، وَأَنْتَ الْبَاطِنُ فَلَيْسَ دُونَكَ شَيْءٌ ، اقْضِ عَنَّا الدَّيْنَ وَأَغْنِنَا مِنَ الفَقْرِ .

Allahumma rabbas-samawatis-sabAA, warabbal-AAarshil-AAatheem, rabbana warabba kulli shay/, faliqal-habbi wannawa, wamunazzilat-tawra, wal-injeel, walfurqan, aAAoothu bika min sharri kulli shayin anta akhithun binasiyatih. Allahumma antal-awwal, falaysa qablaka shay/, wa-antal-akhir, falaysa baAAdaka shay/, wa-antath-thahir falaysa fawqaka shay/, waantal-batin, falaysa doonaka shay/, iqdi AAannad-dayna wa-aghnina minal-faqr.

'O Allah, Lord of the seven heavens and the exalted throne, our Lord and Lord of all things, Splitter of the seed and the date stone, Revealer of the *Tawrah*, the *Injeel* and the *Furqan*, I take refuge in You from the evil of all things You shall seize by the forelock (i.e. You have total mastery over). O Allah, You are The First so there is nothing before You and You are The Last so there is nothing after You. You are *Aththhahir* so there is nothing above You and You are *Al-Batin* so there is nothing closer than You. Settle our debt for us and spare us from poverty.'

-*Tawrah*: The book revealed to Moosa (pbuh).
Injeel: The book revealed to Easa (pbuh).

-*Furqan*: One of the many names of the Quran, means: The Criterion which distinguishes between truth and falsehood.

-*Aththhahir*: Indicates the greatness of His attributes and the insignificance of every single creation in respect to His greatness and Highness, for He is above all of His creation as regards His essence and attributes.

-*Al-Batin*: Indicates His awareness and knowledge of all secrets, of that which is in the hearts and the most intimate of things just as it indicates His closeness and nearness to all in a manner which befits His majesty.

(104)

الـحَمْدُ للهِ الَّذِي أَطْعَمَنا وَسَقانا، وَكَفانا، وَآوانا، فَكَمْ مِمَّنْ لا كافِيَ لَهُ وَلا مُؤْوِي .

Alhamdu lillahil-lathee atAAamana wasaqana, wakafana, wa-awana, fakam mimman la kafiya lahu wala mu/wee.

'All praise is for Allah, Who fed us and gave us drink, and Who is sufficient for us and has sheltered us, for how many have none to suffice them or shelter them.'

(105)

اللّهُمَّ عالِمَ الغَيبِ والشَّهادةِ فاطِرَ السّماواتِ والأرْضِ رَبَّ كُلِّ شَيءٍ وَمَليكَه، أَشْهَدُ أَنْ لا إلهَ إلاّ أَنْت، أَعوذُ بِكَ مِن شَرِّ نَفْسي، وَمِن شَرِّ الشَّيْطانِ وَشِرْكِه، وَأَنْ أَقْتَرِفَ عَلى نَفْسي سوءاً أَوْ أَجُرَّهُ إلى مُسْلِم .

Allahumma AAalimal-ghaybi washshahadah, fatiras-samawati wal-ard, rabba kulli shayin wamaleekah, ashhadu an la ilaha illa ant, aAAoothu bika min sharri nafsee wamin sharrish-

shaytani washirkih, wa-an aqtarifa AAala nafsee soo-an aw ajurrahu ila muslim.

'O Allah, Knower of the seen and the unseen, Creator of the heavens and the earth, Lord and Sovereign of all things I bear witness that none has the right to be worshipped except You. I take refuge in You from the evil of my soul and from the evil and *shirk* of the devil, and from committing wrong against my soul or bringing such upon another Muslim.'

-*shirk*: to associate others with Allah in those things which are specific to Him. This can occur in (1) belief, e.g. to believe that other than Allah has the power to benefit or harm, (2) speech, e.g. to swear by other than Allah and (3) action, e.g. to bow or prostrate to other than Allah.

(106)

'The Prophet ﷺ never used to sleep until he had recited Soorat As-Sajdah (chapter 32) and Soorat Al-Mulk (chapter 67).'

(107)

'If you take to your bed, then perform ablution, lie on your right side and then supplicate:

اللّهُمَّ أَسْلَمْتُ نَفْسي إِلَيْكَ، وَفَوَّضْتُ أَمْري إِلَيْكَ، وَوَجَّهْتُ وَجْهي إِلَيْكَ، وَأَلْجَأْتُ ظَهْـري إِلَيْكَ، رَغْبَةً وَرَهْبَةً إِلَيْكَ، لا مَلْجَأَ وَلا مَنْجا مِنْكَ إِلاَّ إِلَيْكَ، آمَنْتُ بِكِتابِكَ الّذي أَنْزَلْتَ وَبِنَبِيِّكَ الّذي أَرْسَلْت .

Allahumma aslamtu nafsee ilayk, wafawwadtu amree ilayk, wawajjahtu wajhee ilayk, wa-alja/tu

_th_ahree ilayk, raghbatan warahbatan ilayk, l_a_ maljaa wal_a_ manj_a_ minka ill_a_ ilayk, _a_mantu bikit_a_bikal-la_th_ee anzalt, wabinabiyyikal-la_th_ee arsalt.

'O All_a_h, I submit my soul unto You, and I entrust my affair unto You, and I turn my face towards You, and I totally rely on You, in hope and fear of You.Verily there is no refuge nor safe haven from You except with You. I believe in Your Book which You have revealed and in Your Prophet whom You have sent.'

...If you then die, you will die upon the fiṭrah.'

-fiṭrah: the religion of Isl_a_m, the way of Ibr_a_heem (عليه السلام).

29. SUPPLICATION WHEN TURNING OVER DURING THE NIGHT

(108)

_'AA_a_-isha (رضي الله عنها) narrated that the Messenger of All_a_h ﷺ used to say at night if he turned during sleep:_

لا إلهَ إلّا اللهُ الـواحِدُ القَهّار ، رَبُّ السَّمـواتِ وَالأرْضِ وَما بَيْنَهُـما ، العَزيزُ الغَفّار.

La il_a_ha illal-l_a_hul-w_a_hidul-qahh_a_r, rabbus-sam_a_w_a_ti wam_a_ baynahum_a_, alAAazeezul-ghaff_a_r.

'None has the right to be worshipped except All_a_h, The One, _AL-Qahh_a_r_.Lord of the heavens and the Earth and all between them, The Exalted in Might, The Oft-Forgiving.'

-AL-Qahhar: The One Who has subdued all of creation and Whom all of creation are subservient to. All movements occur by His will.

---

30. UPON EXPERIENCING UNREST, FEAR, APPREHENSIVENESS AND THE LIKE DURING SLEEP

(109)

أَعوذُ بِكَلِماتِ اللهِ التّامّاتِ مِن غَضَبِهِ وَعِقابِهِ ، وَشَرِّ عِبادِهِ وَمِنْ هَمَزاتِ الشَّياطينِ وَأَنْ يَحْضُرون.

aAAoothu bikalimatil-lahit-tammat min ghadabih, waAAiqabih, washarri AAibadih, wamin hamazatish-shayateen, wa-an yahduroon.

'I take refuge in the perfect words of Allah from His anger and punishment, and from the evil of His servants, and from the madness and appearance of devils.'

---

31. UPON SEEING A GOOD DREAM OR A BAD DREAM

(110)

'The righteous dream is from Allah and the bad dream is from the devil, so if anyone sees something which pleases him then he should only relate it to one whom he loves...'
Summary of what to do upon having a bad dream:
- *Spit on your left three times*
- *Seek refuge in Allah from shaytan and the evil of what you saw*
- *Do not relate it to anyone*

■ *Turn and sleep on the opposite side to which you were sleeping on previously.*

-**Spit**: A form of spitting comprising mainly of air with little spittle

(111)

■ *Get up and pray if you so desire.*

32. QUNOOT AL-WITR

-**Al-Witr:** Supplication made before or after bowing in the witr prayer

(112)

اللّهُمَّ اهْدِنِي فِيمَنْ هَدَيْت، وَعَافِنِي فِيمَنْ عَافَيْت، وَتَوَلَّنِي فِيمَنْ تَوَلَّيْت، وَبَارِكْ لِي فِيمَا أَعْطَيْت، وَقِنِي شَرَّ ما قَضَيْت، فَإِنَّكَ تَقْضِي وَلَا يُقْضَى عَلَيْك ، إِنَّهُ لَا يَذِلُّ مَنْ والَيْت، [وَلَا يَعِزُّ مَن عَادَيْت]، تَبَارَكْتَ رَبَّنا وَتَعَالَيْت.

Allahummah-dinee feeman hadayt, waAAafinee feeman AAafayt, watawallanee feeman tawallayt, wabarik lee feema aAAtayt, waqinee sharra ma qadayt, fa-innaka taqdee wala yuqda AAalayk, innahu la yathillu man walayt, [wala yaAAizzu man AAadayt], tabarakta rabbana wataAAalayt.

'O Allah, guide me along with those whom You have guided, pardon me along with those whom You have pardoned, be an ally to me along with those whom You are an ally to and bless for me that which You have bestowed. Protect me from the evil You have decreed for verily You decree and none can decree over You.For surety, he whom you show allegiance to is never abased and he whom You take as an enemy is never honoured and mighty. O our Lord, Blessed and Exalted are You.'

-*Evil you have decreed:* All<u>a</u>h does not create pure evil which does not have any good or contain any benefit, wisdom or mercy at all, nor does He punish anyone without having commited a sin. Something can be good in terms of its creation when viewed in a particular perspective and at the same time be evil when viewed in another way.All<u>a</u>h created the devil and by him, He tests His servants, so there are those who hate the devil, fight him and his way and they stand at enmity towards him and his followers and there are others who are at allegiance with the devil and follow his steps. So evil exists in His creatures by His will and wisdom, not in His actions or act of creating.

(113)

اللّهُمَّ إِنِّي أَعوذُ بِرِضاكَ مِنْ سَخَطِكَ، وَبِمُعافاتِكَ مِنْ عُقوبَتِكَ، وَأَعوذُ بِكَ مِنْكَ، لا أُحصي ثَناءً عَلَيْكَ، أَنْتَ كَما أَثْنَيْتَ عَلى نَفْسِكِ.

All<u>a</u>humma innee aAAoothu biridaka min sakhatik, wabimuⱯAafatika min AAuqoobatik, wa-aAAoothu bika mink, la ohsee thana-an AAalayk, anta kama athnayta AAala nafsik.

'O All<u>a</u>h, I take refuge within Your pleasure from Your displeasure and within Your pardon from Your punishment, and I take refuge in You from You. I cannot enumerate Your praise. You are as You have praised Yourself.'

اللّهُمَّ إِيّاكَ نَعْبُدُ، وَلَكَ نُصَلِّي وَنَسْجُدُ، وَإِلَيْكَ نَسْعى وَنَحْفِد، نَرْجو رَحْمَتَكَ، وَنَخْشى عَذابَكَ، إِنَّ عَذابَكَ بِالكافِرين مُلْحَق. اللّهُمَّ إِنّا نَسْتَعِينُكَ وَنَسْتَغْفِرُك، وَنُثْني عَلَيْكَ الخَيْرَ، وَلا نَكْفُرُك، وَنُؤْمِنُ بِك، وَنَخْضَعُ لَكَ وَنَخْلَعُ مَنْ يَكْفُرُك.

Allahumma iyyaka naAAbud, walaka nusallee wanasjud, wa-ilayka nasAAa wanahfid, narjoo rahmatak, wanakhsha AAathabak, inna AAathabaka bilkafireena mulhaq. Allahumma inna nastaAAeenuk, wanastaghfiruk, wanuthnee AAalaykal- khayr, wala nakfuruk, wanu/minu bik, wanakhdaAAu lak wanakhlaAAu man yakfuruk.

'O Allah, it is You we worship, and unto You we pray and prostrate, and towards You we hasten and You we serve. We hope for Your mercy and fear Your punishment, verily Your punishment will fall upon the disbelievers.O Allah, we seek Your aid and ask Your pardon, we praise You with all good and do not disbelieve in You.We believe in You and submit unto You, and we disown and reject those who disbelieve in You.

33. REMEMBRANCE IMMEDIATELY AFTER SALAM OF THE WITR PRAYER

The Messenger of Allah ﷺ would recite (the following chapters) during the witr prayer:

[سَبِّحِ اسْمَ رَبِّكَ الأَعْلَى...]

《Sabbih isma rabbika al-aAAla...》

[Sourat Al-aAAla]

[قُلْ يا أَيُّها الكافِرون...]

《Qul ya ayyuha alkafiroon...》

[Sourat Al-kafiroon]

[قُل هُوَ اللهُ أحد...]

《 Qul huwa Allahu ahad ...》

[Sourat Al-ikhlas]

...after giving salam he would supplicate three times:

سُبْحانَ المَلِكِ القُدّوس (ثلاث مرات)

Subhanal-malikil-quddoos.(three times).

'How perfect The King, The Holy One is.' (three times)

...on the third time he would raise his voice, elongate it and add:

ربِّ الملائكةِ والرّوح

Rabbil-mala-ikati warrooh.

'Lord of the angles and the Rooh (i.e. Jibra-eel).**'**

34. SUPPLICATION FOR ANXIETY AND SORROW

(116)

اللَّهُمَّ إِنِّي عَبْدُكَ ابْنُ عَبْدِكَ ابْنُ أَمَتِكَ نَاصِيَتِي بِيَدِكَ، مَاضٍ فِيَّ حُكْمُكَ، عَدْلٌ فِيَّ قَضَاؤُكَ أَسْأَلُكَ بِكُلِّ اسْمٍ هُوَ لَكَ سَمَّيْتَ بِهِ نَفْسَكَ أَوْ أَنْزَلْتَهُ فِي كِتَابِكَ، أَوْ عَلَّمْتَهُ أَحَداً مِنْ خَلْقِكَ أَوْ

اسْتَأْثَرْتَ بِهِ فِي عِلْمِ الغَيْبِ عِنْدَكَ أَنْ تَجْعَلَ القُرْآنَ رَبِيعَ قَلْبِي، وَنُورَ صَدْرِي وجَلَاءَ حُزْنِي وذَهَابَ هَمِّي.

Allahumma innee AAabduk, ibnu AAabdik, ibnu amatik, nasiyatee biyadik, madin fiyya hukmuk, AAadlun fiyya qada-ok, as-aluka bikulli ismin huwa lak, sammayta bihi nafsak, aw anzaltahu fee kitabik, aw AAallamtahu ahadan min khalqik awis-ta/tharta bihi fee AAilmil-ghaybi AAindak, an tajAAalal-Qurana rabeeAAa qalbee, wanoora sadree, wajalaa huznee wathahaba hammee.

'O Allah, I am Your servant, son of Your servant, son of Your maidservant, my forelock is in Your hand (i.e. You have total mastery over), Your command over me is forever executed and Your decree over me is just. I ask You by every name belonging to You which You named Yourself with, or revealed in Your Book, or You taught to any of Your creation, or You have preserved in the knowledge of the unseen with You, that You make the Quran the life of my heart and the light of my breast, and a departure for my sorrow and a release for my anxiety.'

(117)

اللّهُمَّ إِنِّي أَعُوذُ بِكَ مِنَ الهَمِّ وَ الْحُزْنِ، والعَجْزِ والكَسَلِ والبُخْلِ والجُبْنِ، وضَلْعِ الدَّيْنِ وغَلَبَةِ الرِّجَالِ.

Allahumma innee aAAoothu bika minal-hammi walhuzn, walAAajzi walkasali walbukhli waljubn, wadalAAid-dayni waghalabatir-rijal.

'O Allah, I take refuge in You from anxiety and sorrow, weakness and laziness, miserliness and cowardice, the burden of debts and from being over powered by men.'

35. SUPPLICATION FOR ONE IN DISTRESS

(118)

لَا إِلَهَ إِلَّا اللَّهُ الْعَظِيمُ الْحَلِيمُ، لَا إِلَهَ إِلَّا اللَّهُ رَبُّ الْعَرْشِ الْعَظِيمِ، لَا إِلَهَ إِلَّا اللَّهُ رَبُّ السَّمَوَاتِ وَرَبُّ الأَرْضِ وَرَبُّ الْعَرْشِ الكَرِيم .

La ilaha illal-lahul-AAatheemul-haleem, la ilaha illal-lahu rabbul-AAarshil-AAatheem, la ilaha illal-lahu rabbus-samawati warabbul-ardi warabbul-AAarshil-kareem.

'None has the right to be worshipped except Allah Forbearing. None has the right to be worshipped except Allah, Lord of the magnificent throne. None has the right to be worshipped except Allah, Lord of the heavens, Lord of the Earth and Lord of the noble throne.'

(119)

اللَّهُمَّ رَحْمَتَكَ أَرْجُو فَلَا تَكِلْنِي إِلَى نَفْسِي طَرْفَةَ عَيْنٍ، وَأَصْلِحْ لِي شَأْنِي كُلَّهُ لَا إِلَهَ إِلَّا أَنْتَ .

Allahumma rahmataka arjoo fala takilnee ila nafsee tarfata AAayn, wa-aslih lee sha/nee kullah, la ilaha illa ant.

'O Allah, it is Your mercy that I hope for, so do not leave me in charge of my affairs even for a blink of an eye and rectify for me all of my affairs. None has the right to be worshipped except You.'

(120)

لَا إِلَهَ إِلَّا أَنْتَ سُبْحانَكَ إِنِّي كُنْتُ مِنَ الظّالِمِين.

**La ilaha illa anta subhanaka innee kuntu mina_th-_
_th_alimeen.**

'None has the right to be worshipped except You. How perfect You are, verily I was among the wrong-doers.'

(121)

اللهُ اللهُ رَبِّي لا أُشْرِكُ بِهِ شَيْئاً.

Alla_hu All_ahu rabbi la oshriku bihi shay_a_.

'Alla_h_, Alla_h_ is my Lord, I do not associate anything with Him.'

36. UPON ENCOUNTERING AN ENEMY OR THOSE OF AUTHORITY

(122)

اللّهُمَّ إِنا نَجْعَلُكَ في نُحورِهِم، وَنَعوذُ بِكَ مِنْ شُرورِهِمْ .

Alla_h_umma inn_a_ najAAaluka fee nu_h_oorihim wanaAAoo_th_u bika min shuroorihim.

'O Alla_h_, we place You before them and we take refuge in You from their evil.'

(123)

اللّهُمَّ أَنْتَ عَضُدِي، وَأَنْتَ نَصيري، بِكَ أَجولُ وَبِكَ أَصولُ وَبِكَ أُقاتِل .

Allahumma anta AAadudee, wa-anta naseeree, bika ajoolu wabika asoolu wabika oqatil.

'O Allah, You are my supporter and You are my helper, by You I move and by You I attack and by You I battle.'

(124)

حَسْبُنا اللهُ وَنِعْمَ الوَكيل.

Hasbunal-lahu waniAAmal-wakeel.

'Allah is sufficient for us, and how fine a trustee (He is).'

37. SUPPLICATION FOR ONE AFFLICTED WITH DOUBT IN HIS FAITH

(125)

- *He should seek refuge in Allah*
- *He should renounce that which is causing such doubt.*

(126)

- *He should say*:

آمَنْتُ بِاللهِ وَرُسُلِه.

Amantu billahi warusulih.

'I have believed in Allah and His Messengers.'

(127)

- *He should also recite the following verse*:

─────────

73

﴿هُوَ الأَوَّلُ، وَالآخِرُ، وَالظَّاهِرُ، وَالْبَاطِنُ، وَهُوَ بِكُلِّ شَيءٍ عَلِيم﴾ .

﴾Huwa al-awwalu, waal-akhiru, waalththahiru waalbatinu wahuwa bikulli shayin AAaleem﴿.

'He is The First and The Last, Aththahir and Al-Batin and He knows well all things.'

-Aththahir: Indicates the greatness of His attributes and the insignificance of every single creation in respect to His greatness and Highness, for He is above all of His creation as regards His essence and attributes.

-Al-Batin: Indicates His awareness and knowledge of all secrets, of that which is in the hearts and the most intimate of things just as it indicates His closeness and nearness to all in a manner which befits His majesty.

38. SETTLING A DEBT

(128)

اللّهُمَّ اكْفِنِي بِحَلالِكَ عَنْ حَرَامِكَ، وَأَغْنِنِي بِفَضْلِكَ عَمَّنْ سِوَاكَ .

Allahummak-finee bihalalika AAan haramik, wa-aghninee bifadlika AAamman siwak.

'O Allah, make what is lawful enough for me, as opposed to what is unlawful, and spare me by Your grace, of need of others.'

(129)

اللّهُمَّ إِنِّي أَعُوذُ بِكَ مِنَ الهَمِّ وَ الْحُزْنِ، والعَجْزِ والكَسَلِ والبُخْلِ والجُبْنِ، وضَلْعِ الدَّيْنِ وغَلَبَةِ الرِّجالِ.

Allahumma innee aAAoothu bika minal-hammi walhuzn, walAAajzi walkasal, walbukhl, waljubn, wadalAAid-dayni waghalabatir-rijal.

'O Allah, I take refuge in You from anxiety and sorrow, weakness and laziness, miserliness and cowardice, the burden of debts and from being over powered by men.'

39. SUPPLICATION FOR ONE AFFLICATED BY WHISPERINGS IN PRAYER OR RECITATION
(130)

'othman Ibn Al-AAas ◈ narrated: I said 'O Messenger of Allah, verily the devil comes between me and my prayer and recitation making me confused' The Messenger of Allah ﷺ replied 'That is a devil called Khanzab, so if you sense his presence then seek refuge in Allah from him and spit (A form of spitting comprising mainly of air with little spittle) on your left side three times.'

40. SUPPLICATION FOR ONE WHOSE AFFAIRS HAVE BECOME DIFFICULT
(131)

اللّهُمَّ لا سَهْلَ إِلاّ ما جَعَلْتَهُ سَهْلاً، وَأَنْتَ تَجْعَلُ الْحَزَنَ إِذا شِئْتَ سَهْلاً.

Allahumma la sahla illa ma jaAAaltahu sahla, wa-anta tajAAalul- hazana in shi/ta sahla.

'O Allah, there is no ease except in that which You
have made easy, and You make the difficulty, if You
wish, easy.'

41. UPON COMMITTING A SIN
(132)

*'Any servant who commits a sin and as a result, performs
ablution, prays two units of prayer (i.e. two rakAAas) and
then seeks Allah's forgiveness, Allah would forgive him.'*

42. SUPPLICATION FOR EXPELLING THE DEVIL AND HIS WHISPERINGS
(133)

■ *Seeking refuge from him.*

(134)

■ *The athan (call to prayer).*

(135)

■ *Recitation of the Quran and the authentic texts of
remembrance and supplications.*

*e.g. 'Do not make your homes like the graveyards, indeed
the devils flee from the house in which soorat Al-Baqarah
has been read'* related by Muslim 1/539, also
supplication and remembrance for the morning &
evening, before sleep, when getting up, entering and
leaving the toilet, entering and leaving the mosque,
the recitation of ayat Al-kursiyy and the last two
verses of soorat Al-Baqarah before sleeping, the
athan...etc.

43. SUPPLICATION WHEN STRICKEN WITH A MISHAP OR OVERTAKEN BY AN AFFAIR

(136)

'The strong believer is better and more beloved to Allah, than the weak believer and there is goodness in both. Strive for that which will benefit you ,seek help from Allah and do not despair. If a mishap should happen to befall you then do not say 'If only I had acted…such and such would have happened'. Rather, say:

قَدَّرَ اللّٰهُ وَما شـاءَ فَعَـل .

Qaddaral-lah, wama shaa faAAal.

'Allah has decreed and what He wills, He does.'
*…for verily '**If**' lets in the work of the devil.'*

(137)

Indeed Allah تعالى *rebukes due to negligence and slackness, but take to determination and caution, and if a matter should overtake you then say:*

حَسْـبِيَ اللّٰهُ وَنِـعْمَ الوَكيـل .

Hasbiyal-lah, waniAAmal-wakeel.

'Allah is sufficient for me, and how fine a trustee (He is).'

44. PLACING CHILDEN UNDER ALLAH'S PROTECTION

(138)

Ibn AAabbas reluted that the Messenger of Allah ﷺ *used to commend Al-Hasan and Al-Husayn to Allah's protection, saying:*

أُعِيذُكُمَا بِكَلِمَاتِ اللهِ التَّامَّة، مِنْ كُلِّ شَيْطَانٍ وَهَامَّة، وَمِنْ كُلِّ عَيْنٍ لامَّة .

OAAeethukuma bikalimatil-lahit-tammah, min kulli shaytanin wahammah, wamin kulli AAaynin lammah.

'I commend you two to the protection of Allah's perfect words from every devil, vermin, and every evil eye.'

45. WHEN VISITING THE SICK

(139)

When the Prophet ﷺ would enter upon a sick person, he would say:

لا بَأْسَ طَهُورٌ إِنْ شَاءَ اللهُ .

La ba/sa tahoorun in shaal-lah.

'Never mind, may it (the sickness) be a purification, if Allah wills.'

(140)

'Any Muslim servant who visits a sick person whose prescribed moment of death has not arrived and supplicates seven times:

أَسْأَلُ اللهَ العَظِيمَ، رَبَّ العَرْشِ العَظِيمَ أَنْ يَشْفِيكَ .(سبع مرات)

Asalul-lahal-AAatheem rabbal-AAarshil-AAatheem an yashfeek (7 times).

'I ask Allah The Supreme, Lord of the magnificent throne to cure you'. (7 times)
...he (the sick person) will be cured.'

46. EXCELLENCE OF VISITING THE SICK
(141)

'Ali Ibn Abee Talib ☀ *related that he heard the Messenger of Allah* ☀ *say: 'If a man calls on his sick Muslim brother, it is as if he walks reaping the fruits of Paradise until he sits, and when he sits he is showered in mercy, and if this was in the morning, seventy thousand angles send prayers upon him until the evening, and if this was in the evening, seventy thousand angles send prayers upon him until the morning.'*

47. SUPPLICATION OF THE SICK WHO HAVE RENOUNCED ALL HOPE OF LIFE
(142)

اَللّهُمَّ اغْفِرْ لِي وَارْحَمْنِي وَأَلْحِقْنِي بِالرَّفِيقِ الأَعْلَى .

Allahummagh-fir lee, warhamnee wa-alhiqnee birrafeeqil-aAAla.

'O Allah, forgive me, have mercy upon me and unite me with the higher companions.'

Refer to the Quran, chapter 4, verse: 69.

(143)

AAaishah رضي الله عنها *related that the Prophet* ☀ *(during his illness in which he passed away) would dip his hands in water and then he would wipe his face and say:*

لَا إِلَهَ إِلَّا اللهَ، إِنَّ لِلمَوْتِ لَسَكَرَات .

La ilaha illal-lah, inna lilmawti lasakarat.

'None has the right to be worshipped except Allah, death does indeed contain agony.'

(144)

لَا إِلَهَ إِلاَّ اللّهُ وَاللّهُ أَكْبَرُ، لَا إِلَهَ إِلاَّ اللّهُ وَحْدَهُ لَا شَرِيكَ لَهُ، لَا

إِلَهَ إِلاَّ اللّهُ لَهُ الْمُلْكُ وَلَهُ الْحَمْدُ، لَا إِلَهَ إِلاَّ اللّهُ وَلَا حَوْلَ وَلَا

قُوَّةَ إِلاَّ بِاللّهِ.

La ilaha illal-lah, wallahu akbar, la ilaha illal-lahu wahdah, la shareeka lah, la ilaha illal-lahu lahul-mulku walahul-hamd, la ilaha illal-lah, wala hawla wala quwwata illa billah.

'None has the right to be worshipped except Allah and Allah is the greatest. None has the right to be worshipped except Allah, alone. None has the right to be worshipped except Allah, alone, without partner. None has the right to be worshipped except Allah, to Him belongs all sovereignty and praise. None has the right to be worshipped except Allah and there is no might and no power except with Allah.'

48. INSTRUCTION FOR THE ONE NEARING DEATH

i.e. those around the sick should instruct and encourage him to say the shahadah.

(145)

'He whose last words are:

لا إلهَ إلاَّ اللّه.

La ilaha illal-lah.

'None has the right to be worshipped except Allah.'
...will enter Paradise.'

49. SUPPLICATION FOR ONE AFFLICTED BY A CALAMITY

(146)

إِنّا لِلّهِ وَإِنّا إِلَيْهِ راجِعـون ، اللهُـمّ أْجُـرْني في مُصيبَتي، وَاخْلُفْ

لي خَيْـراً مِنْها.

Inna lillahi wa-inna ilayhi rajiAAoon, allahumma/-jurnee fee museebatee wakhluf lee khayran minha.

'To Allah we belong and unto Him is our return.O Allah, recompense me for my affliction and replace it for me with something better.'

50. WHEN CLOSING THE EYES OF THE DECEASED

(147)

اللهُـمّ اغْفِـرْ لِـفُلان باسـمه- وَارْفَعْ دَرَجَتَـهُ في المَهْـدِيـين ،

وَاخْـلُفْهُ في عَقِبِهِ في الغابِرين، وَاغْفِـرْ لَنـا وَلَهُ يا رَبَّ

العـالَمين، وَافْسَـحْ لَهُ في قَبْـرِهِ وَنَوِّرْ لَهُ فيه .

Allahummagh-fir li-name the dead- warfaAA darajatahu fil-mahdiyyeen, wakhlufhu fee AAaqibihi fil-ghabireen, waghfir lana walahu ya rabbal-AAalameen wafsah lahu fee qabrih, wanawwir lahu feeh.

'O Allah, forgive -here the name of the deceased is mentioned- and raise his rank among the rightly guided, and be a successor to whom he has left behind, and forgive us and him O Lord of the worlds. Make spacious his grave and illuminate it for him.'

-*A successor:* one who succeeds another due to the latter's absence or death. This is the correct meaning of the word *khaleefah*; thus, it is incorrect to believe that Adam is the khaleefah (*vicegerent,* as is commonly translated) of Allah on earth because Allah is never absent, and will never die. This supplication proves the correct understanding of this term and shows that Allah succeeds us and guards whom we leave behind when we die or are absent. (also refer to supplication #198)

51. SUPPLICATION FOR THE DECEASED AT THE FUNERAL PRAYER

(148)

اللهُمَّ اغْفِرْ لَهُ وَارْحَمْهُ ، وَعافِهِ وَاعْفُ عَنْهُ ، وَأَكْرِمْ نُزُلَهُ ، وَوَسِّعْ مُدْخَلَهُ ، وَاغْسِلْهُ بِالْمَاءِ وَالثَّلْجِ وَالْبَرَدْ ، وَنَقِّهِ مِنَ الْخَطَايَا كَمَا نَقَّيْتَ الثَّوْبُ الأَبْيَضُ مِنَ الدَّنَسِ ، وَأَبْدِلْهُ دَاراً خَيْراً مِنْ دَارِهِ ، وَأَهْلاً خَيْراً مِنْ أَهْلِهِ ، وَزَوْجَاً خَيْراً مِنْ زَوْجِهِ ، وَأَدْخِلْهُ الْجُنَّةَ ، وَأَعِذْهُ مِنْ عَذَابِ الْقَبْرِ وَعَذَابِ النَّارِ .

Allahummagh-fir lahu warhamh, waAAafihi, waAAfu AAanh, wa-akrim nuzulah, wawassiAA mudkhalah, waghsilhu bilma-i waththalji walbarad, wanaqqihi minal-khataya kama naqqaytath-thawbal-abyada minad-danas, wa-abdilhu daran khayran min darih, wa-ahlan khayran min ahlih wazawjan khayran min zawjih, wa-adkhilhul-jannah, wa-aAAithhu min AAathabil-qabr, waAAAathabin-nar.

'O Allah, forgive and have mercy upon him, excuse him and pardon him, and make honourable his reception. Expand his entry, and cleanse him with water, snow, and ice, and purify him of sin as a white robe is purified of filth. Exchange his home for a better home, and his family for a better family, and his spouse for a better spouse. Admit him into the Garden, protect him from the punishment of the grave and the torment of the Fire.'

(149)

اللهُمَّ اغْفِرْ لِحَيِّنا وَمَيِّتِنا وَشاهِدِنا ، وَغائِبِنا ، وَصَغيرِنا وَكَبيرِنا ، وَذَكَرِنا وَأُنْثانا . اللهُمَّ مَنْ أَحْيَيْتَهُ مِنّا فَأَحْيِهِ عَلى الإِسْلام ،وَمَنْ تَوَفَّيْتَهُ مِنّا فَتَوَفَّهُ عَلى الإِيمانِ ، اللهُمَّ لا تَحْرِمْنا أَجْرَهُ ، وَلا تُضِلَّنا بَعْدَهُ .

Allahummagh-fir lihayyina wamayyitina washahidina, wagha-ibina, wasagheerina wakabeerina, wathakarina wa-onthana. Allahumma man ahyaytahu minna fa-ahyihi AAalal-islam, waman tawaffaytahu minna fatawaffahu AAalal-

eem_a_n, all_a_humma l_a_ ta_h_rimn_a_ ajrah, wal_a_
tu_d_illan_a_ baAAdah.

'O All_a_h, forgive our living and our dead, those
present and those absent, our young and our old, our
males and our females. O All_a_h, whom amongst us
You keep alive, then let such a life be upon Isl_a_m,
and whom amongst us You take unto Yourself, then
let such a death be upon faith. O All_a_h, do not
deprive us of his reward and do not let us stray after
him.'

(150)

اللهُمَّ إِنَّ فُلانَ بْنَ فُلانٍ فِي ذِمَّتِكَ ، وَحَبْلِ جِـوارِكَ ، فَقِهِ مِنْ
فِتْنَةِ الْقَبْرِ وَعَذابِ النّـارِ ، وَأَنْتَ أَهْلُ الْوَفاءِ وَالْحَقِّ ، فَاغْفِرْ
لَهُ وَارْحَمْـهُ ، إِنَّكَ أَنْتَ الغَفورُ الرَّحيم .

All_a_humma inna -name the dead- fee _th_immatik,
wa_h_abli jiw_a_rik, faqihi min fitnatil-qabr
waAAa_th_abin-n_a_r, wa-anta ahlul-wafa/, wal_h_aq,
faghfir lahu war_h_amh, innaka antal-ghafoorur-
raheem.

'O All_a_h, so-and-so is under Your care and protection
so protect him from the trial of the grave and torment
of the Fire. Indeed You are faithful and truthful.
Forgive and have mercy upon him, surely You are
The Oft-Forgiving, The Most-Merciful.'

(151)

اللهُمَّ عَبْدُكَ وَابْنُ أَمَتِكَ، احْتَاجَ إلى رَحْمَتِكَ، وَأَنْتَ غَنِيٌّ عَنْ عَذابِهِ، إنْ كانَ مُحْسِناً فَزِدْ في حَسَناتِهِ، وَإنْ كانَ مُسيئاً فَتَجاوَزْ عَنْه.

Allahumma AAabduka wabnu amatik, ihtaja ila rahmatik, wa-anta ghaniyyun AAan AAathabih, in kana muhsinan fazid fee hasanatih, wa-in kana museean fatajawaz AAanh.

'O Allah, Your servant and the son of Your maidservant is in need of Your mercy and You are without need of his punishment. If he was righteous then increase his reward and if he was wicked then look over his sins.'

52. SUPPLICATION FOR THE ADVANCEMENT OF REWARD DURING THE FUNERAL PRAYER

This supplication is made when the deceased is a baby/child (i.e. one not having reached the age of puberty).

(152)

After seeking forgiveness for the deceased, one can say:

اللهُمَّ اجْعَلْهُ فَرَطاً وَذُخْراً لِوالِدَيه، وَشَفيعاً مُجاباً، اللهُمَّ ثَقِّلْ بِهِ مَوازينَهُما، وَأَعْظِمْ بِهِ أُجورَهُما، وَألْحِقْهُ بِصالِحِ المؤمِنين، وَاجْعَلْهُ في كَفالَةِ إِبْراهيم، وَقِهِ بِرَحْمَتِكَ عَذابَ الجَحيم.

Allahummaj-AAalhu faratan, wathukhran liwalidayh, washafeeAAan mujaban. Allahumma thaqqil bihi mawazeenahuma wa-aAAthim bihi ojoorahuma, wa-alhiqhu bisalihil-mu/mineen, wajAAalhu fee kafalati Ibraheem, waqihi birahmatika AAathabal-jaheem.

'O Allah, make him a preceding reward and a stored treasure for his parents, and an answered intercessor. O Allah, through him, make heavy their scales and magnify their reward. Unite him with the righteous believers, place him under the care of Ibraheem, and protect him by Your mercy from the torment of Hell.'

(153)

Al-Hasan used to recite the opening chapter of the Quran (i.e. AL-Fatihah) over the child and then supplicates:

اللهُمَّ اجْعَلْهُ لَنا فَرَطاً، وَسَلَفاً وَأَجْراً.

Allahummaj-AAalhu lana farata, wasalafan wa-ajra.

'O Allah, make him a preceding reward, a prepayment and a recompense for us.'

53. CONDOLENCE

(154)

إِنَّ للهِ ما أَخَذ، وَلَهُ ما أَعْطى، وَكُلُّ شَيءٍ عِنْدَهُ بِأَجَلٍ مُسَمَّى .فَلْتَصْبِر وَلْتَحْتَسِب.

Inna lillahi ma akhath, walahu ma aAAta, wakullu shayin AAindahu bi-ajalin musamma...faltasbir waltahtasib.

'Verily to Allah, belongs what He took and to Him belongs what He gave, and everything with Him has an appointed time…and then he ﷺ ordered for her to be patient and hope for Allah's reward.'

The words (**faltasbir waltahtasib**) are commands in the feminine 3rd person form, so they will need to be changed in respect to whom is being addressed.
…and one can also say:

أَعْظَمَ اللّٰهُ أَجْرَكِ، وَأَحْسَنَ عَزَاءَ كِ، وَغَفَرَ لِمَيِّتِكِ.

aAA*th*amal-lahu ajrak, wa-ahsana AAaza̠ak, waghafara limayyitik.

'May Allah magnify your reward, make better your solace and forgive your deceased.'

This is the saying of some of the scholars, *not* a hadeeth.

54. PLACING THE DECEASED IN THE GRAVE
(155)

بِسْـمِ اللّٰهِ وَعَلَى سُـنَّةِ رَسـولِ اللّٰه .

Bismil-lahi waAAala sunnati rasoolil-lah.

'In the name of Allah and upon the sunnah of the Messenger of Allah.'

55. AFTER BURYING THE DECEASED
(156)

'After the Prophet ﷺ would bury the deceased he would stand by the grave and say: 'Seek forgiveness for your brother and pray that he remains firm, for he is now being questioned'.'

56. VISITING THE GRAVES

(157)

السَّلامُ عَلَيْكُمْ أَهْلَ الدِّيارِ مِنَ المؤمنيـنَ وَالْمُسْلِمِين، وَإِنَّا إِنْ شاءَ اللهُ بِكُـمْ لاحِقون، نَسْأَلُ اللهَ لنا وَلَكُمُ العافِيَة.

Assalamu AAalaykum ahlad-diyari minal-mu/mineena walmuslimeen, wa-inna in sha al-lahu bikum lahiqoon, nas-alul-laha lana walakumul-AAafiyah.

'Peace be upon you all, O inhabitants of the graves, amongst the believers and the Muslims. Verily we will, Allah willing, be united with you, we ask Allah for well-being for us and you.'

57. PRAYER SAID DURING A WIND STORM

(158)

اللّهُـمَّ إِنِّي أَسْأَلُكَ خَيْـرَها، وَأَعوذُ بِكَ مِنْ شَـرِّها.

Allahumma innee as-aluka khayraha wa-aAAoothu bika min sharriha.

'O Allah, I ask You for it's goodness and I take refuge with You from it's evil.'

(159)

اللّهُـمَّ إِنِّي أَسْأَلُكَ خَيْـرَها، وَخَيْـرَ ما فيها، وَخَيْـرَ ما أُرْسِلَت بِهِ، وَأَعـوذُ بِكَ مِنْ شَـرِّها، وَشَـرِّ ما فيها، وَشَـرِّ ما أُرْسِلَتْ بِهِ.

Allahumma innee as-aluka khayraha wakhayra ma feeha, wakhayra ma orsilat bih, wa-aAAoothu bika min sharriha, washarri ma feeha washarri ma orsilat bih.

'O Allah, I ask You for it's goodness, the good within it, and the good it was sent with, and I take refuge with You from it's evil, the evil within it, and from the evil it was sent with.'

58. SUPPLICATION UPON HEARING THUNDER
(160)

When AAabdullah Ibn Az-Zubayr ⚘ used to hear thunder he would stop talking and say:

سُبْحانَ الّذي يُسَبِّحُ الرَّعْدُ بِحَمْدِهِ، وَالملائِكةُ مِنْ خِيفَته.

Subhanal-lathee yusabbihur-raAAdu bihamdih, walmala-ikatu min kheefatih.

'How perfect He is, (The One) Whom the thunder declares His perfection with His praise, as do the angles out of fear of Him.'

59. SUPPLICATION FOR RAIN
(161)

اللّهُمَّ اسْقِنا غَيْثاً مُغِيثاً مَرِيئاً مُرِيعاً، نافِعاً غَيْرَ ضار، عاجِلاً غَيْرَ آجِل.

Allahummas-qina ghaythan mugheethan maree-an mureeAAan, nafiAAan, ghayra dar, AAajilan ghayra ajil.

'O Allah, send upon us helpful, wholesome and healthy rain, beneficial not harmful rain, now, not later.'

(162)

اللّهُمَّ أَغِثْنـا، اللّهُمَّ أَغِثْنـا، اللّهُمَّ أَغِثْنـا.

Allahumma aghithna, allahumma aghithna, allahumma aghithna.

'O Allah, relieve us, O Allah, relieve us, O Allah, relieve us.'

(163)

اللّهُمَّ اسْقِ عِبادَكَ وَبَهـائِمَكَ، وَانْشُـرْ رَحْمَتَكَ وَأَحْيِي بَلَدَكَ المَيِّت.

Allahummas-qi AAibadak, wabaha-imak, wanshur rahmatak, wa-ahyi baladakal-mayyit.

'O Allah, provide water for Your servants and Your cattle, spread out Your mercy and resurrect Your dead land.'

60. SUPPLICATION SAID WHEN IT RAINS

(164)

اللّهُمَّ صَيِّباً نافِعاً.

Allahumma sayyiban nafiAAa.

'O Allah, may it be a beneficial rain cloud.'

61. AFTER RAINFALL

(165)

مُطِـرْنا بِفَضْـلِ اللهِ وَرَحْمَتِه.

Mutirna bifadlil-lahi warahmatih.

'We have been given rain by the grace and mercy of Allah.'

---

62. ASKING FOR CLEAR SKIES

(166)

اللّهُمَّ حَوالَيْنا وَلا عَلَيْنا، اللّهُمَّ عَلى الآكـامِ وَالظِّـراب، وَبُطـونِ الأوْدِية، وَمَنـابِتِ الشَّجر .

Allahumma hawalayna wala AAalayna, allahumma AAalal-akami waththirab, wabutoonil-awdiyah, wamanabitish-shajar.

'O Allah, let the rain fall around us and not upon us, O Allah, (let it fall) on the pastures, hills, valleys and the roots of trees.'

63. UPON SIGHTING THE CRESCENT MOON

(167)

اللهُ أَكْبَر، اللّهُمَّ أَهِلَّهُ عَلَيْنا بِالأمْنِ وَالإيمانِ، والسَّلامَةِ والإسْلام، وَالتَّوْفيـقِ لِما تُحِـبُّ وَتَرضى، رَبُّنـا وَرَبُّكَ الله .

Allahu akbar, allahumma ahillahu AAalayna bil-amni wal-eeman, wassalamati wal-islam, wattawfeeiqi lima tuhibbu watarda, rabbuna warabbukal-lah.

'Allah is the greatest. O Allah, let the crescent loom above us in safety, faith, peace, and Islam, and in agreement with all that You love and pleases You. Our Lord and your Lord is Allah.'

64. UPON BREAKING FAST

(168)

ذَهَبَ الظَّمَأُ، وَابْتَلَّتِ العُروقِ، وَثَبَتَ الأجْرُ إنْ شاءَ الله .

<u>Th</u>ahaba<u>th</u>-<u>th</u>ama-o   wabtallatil-AAuʋouq, watha batal-ajru in <u>sh</u>aal-la<u>h</u>.

'The thirst has gone and the veins are quenched, and reward is confirmed, if Alla<u>h</u> wills.'

(169)

'AAabdulla<u>h</u> Ibn AAamr Ibn Al-AA<u>as</u> ❀ related that the Messenger of Alla<u>h</u> ﷺ said: 'Indeed the fasting person has at the time of breaking fast, a supplication which is not rejected'.

Ibn Abee Mulaykah رحمه الله *said: 'I Heard AAabdulla<u>h</u> Ibn AAomar say when he broke his fast:*

اللّٰهُمَّ إِنِّي أَسْأَلُكَ بِرَحْمَتِكَ الَّتِي وَسِعَت كُلَّ شيء، أَنْ تَغْفِرَ لي .

Alla<u>h</u>umma inne as-aluka birahmatikal-latee wasiAAat kulla shay, an taghfira lee.

'O Alla<u>h</u>, I ask You by Your mercy which envelopes all things, that You forgive me.'

65. SUPPLICATION BEFORE EATING

(170)

'When you are about to eat, you should say:

بِسْمِ الله .

Bismil-la<u>h</u>.

'In the name of Alla<u>h</u>'

...and if you forget to say it before starting, then you should say (when you remember):

بِسْمِ اللّٰهِ في أَوَّلِهِ وَآخِرِهِ .

Bismil-la<u>h</u>i fee awwalihi wa-<u>a</u>khirih.

'In the name of Alla<u>h</u> in it's beginning and end.'

'Whomever Allah feeds, should say:

اللّهُـمَّ بارِكْ لَنا فيهِ وَأَطْعِمْنا خَيْراً مِنْـه.

Allahumma barik lana feehi wa-atAAimna khayran minh.

'O Allah, bless it for us and feed us better than it.'

....and whomever Allah gives milk to drink should say:

اللّهُـمَّ بارِكْ لَنا فيهِ وَزِدْنا مِنْه.

Allahumma barik lana feehi wazidna minh.

'O Allah, bless it for usand give us more of it.'

66. UPON COMPLETING THE MEAL

(172)

الْحَمْدُ لِلّهِ الَّذي أَطْعَمَني هـذا وَرَزَقَنيهِ مِنْ غَيْرِ حَوْلٍ مِنِّي وَلا قُوَّة .

Alhamdu lillahil-lathee atAAamanee hatha warazaqaneehi min ghayri hawlin minnee wala quwwah.

'All praise is for Allah who fed me this and provided it for me without any might nor power from myself.'

(173)

الْحَمْدُ لِلّهِ حَمْداً كَثيراً طَيِّباً مُبارَكاً فيهِ، غَيْرَ مَكْفِيٍّ وَلا مُوَدَّعٍ وَلا مُسْتَغْنىً عَنْهُ رَبُّنا .

Alhamdu lillahi hamdan katheeran tayyiban mubarakan feeh, ghayra makfiyyin wala

muwaddaAAin, wala mustaghnan AAanhu rabbuna.

'Allah be praised with an abundant beautiful blessed praise, a never-ending praise, a praise which we will never bid farewell to and an indispensable praise, He is our Lord.'

There are other views as regards to the understanding of this supplication, from them: *Allah be praised with an abundant beautiful blessed praise. He is The One Who is sufficient, feeds and is not fed. The One Who is longed for, along with that which is with Him and The One Who is needed, He is our Lord.'*

67. SUPPLICATION OF THE GUEST FOR THE HOST

(174)

اللّٰهُمَّ بارِكْ لَهُمْ فِيا رَزَقْتَهُم، وَاغْفِرْ لَهُمْ وَارْحَمْهُمْ.

Allahumma barik lahum feema razaqtahum, waghfir lahum warhamhum.

'O Allah, bless for them, that which You have provided them, forgive them and have mercy upon them.'

68. SUPPLICATION SAID TO ONE OFFERING A DRINK OR TO ONE WHO INTENDED TO DO THAT

(175)

اللّٰهُمَّ أَطْعِمْ مَنْ أَطْعَمَنِي، وَاسْقِ مَنْ سقاني.

Allahumma atAAim man atAAamanee wasqi man saqanee.

'O Allah, feed him who fed me, and provide with drink him who provided me with drink.'

69. SUPPLICATION SAID WHEN BREAKING FAST IN SOMEONE'S HOME
(176)

أَفْطَرَ عِنْدَكُمُ الصّائِمونَ وَأَكَلَ طَعامَكُمُ الأبْرار، وَصَلَّتْ عَلَيْكُمُ الملائِكَة.

Aftara AAindakumus-sa-imoon, wa-akala taAAamakumul-abrar, wasallat AAalaykumul-mala-ikah.

'May the fasting break their fast in your home, and may the dutiful and pious eat your food, and may the angles send prayers upon you.'

70. SUPPLICATION SAID BY ONE FASTING WHEN PRESENTED WITH FOOD AND DOES NOT BREAK HIS FAST
(177)

'If you are invited (to a meal) then answer. If you happen to be fasting, then supplicate (for those present) and if you are not fasting, then eat.'

71. SUPPLICATION SAID UPON SEEING THE EARLY OR PREMATURE FRUIT
(178)

اللّهُمَّ بارِكْ لَنا في ثَمَرِنا، وَبارِكْ لَنا في مَدينَتِنا، وَبارِكْ لَنا في صاعِنا، وَبارِكْ لَنا في مُدِّنا.

Allahumma barik lana fee thamarina, wabarik lana fee madeenatina, wabarik lana fee saAAina wabarik lana fee muddina.

'O Allah, bless our fruit for us, bless our town for us, bless our *saAA* for us and bless our *mudd* for us.'

-A *saAA* is equivalent to four *mudds* and a *mudd* is equivalent to a dry measure of an average man's two palms.

72. SUPPLICATION SAID UPON SNEEZING
(179)

'When one of you sneezes he should say:

الْحَمْدُ لِلَّهِ.

Alhamdu lillah.

'All praise if for Allah.'
...and his brother or companion should say to him:

يَرْحَمُكَ الله.

Yarhamukal-lah.

'May Allah have mercy upon you.'
...and he (i.e. the one who sneezed) replies back to him:

يَهْديكُمُ اللّهُ وَيُصْلِحُ بالَكُمْ.

Yahdeekumul-lahu wayuslihu balakum.

'May Allah guide you and rectify your condition.'

73. SUPPLICATION SAID TO THE NEWLYWED

(180)

بَارَكَ اللّهُ لَكَ، وَبَارَكَ عَلَيْكَ، وَجَمَعَ بَيْنَكُمَا فِي خَيْرٍ .

Barakal-lahu lak, wabaraka AAalayk, wajamaAAa baynakuma fee khayr.

'May Allah bless for you (your spouse) and bless you, and may He unite both of you in goodness.'

74. THE GROOM'S SUPPLICATION ON THE WEDDING NIGHT OR WHEN BUYING AN ANIMAL

(181)

when you marry a woman or buy a maidservant, you should say:

اللّهُمَّ إِنِّي أَسْأَلُكَ خَيْرَها، وَخَيْرَ مَا جَبَلْتَهَا عَلَيْهِ، وَأَعُوذُ بِكَ مِنْ شَرِّها، وَشَرِّ مَا جَبَلْتَهَا عَلَيْهِ.

Allahumma innee as-aluka khayraha wakhayra ma jabaltaha AAalayh, wa-aAAoothu bika min sharriha washarri ma jabaltaha AAalayh.

'O Allah, I ask You for the goodness within her and the goodness that you have made her inclined towards, and I take refuge with You from the evil within her and the evil that you have made her inclined towards.'

…and if you buy a camel, then you should take hold of it's hump and say likewise.'

75. SUPPLICATION BEFORE SEXUAL INTERCOURSE

(182)

بِسْمِ اللهِ اللّٰهُمَّ جَنِّبْنا الشَّيْطانَ، وَجَنِّبِ الشَّيْطانَ ما رَزَقْتَنا.

Bismil-lah, allahumma jannibnash-shaytan, wajannibish-shaytana ma razaqtana.

'In the name of Allah. O Allah, keep the devil away from us and keep the devil away from what you have blessed us with.'

---

76. WHEN ANGRY

(183)

أَعوذُ بِاللهِ مِنَ الشَّيْطانِ الرَّجيمِ .

aAAoothu billahi minash-shaytanir-rajeem.

'I take refuge with Allah from the accursed devil.'

---

77. SUPPLICATION SAID UPON SEEING SOMEONE IN TRIAL OR TRIBULATION

This supplication is to be said to one's self, not directly to the one in trial or tribulation.

(184)

الْحَمْدُ للهِ الَّذي عافاني مِمّا ابْتَلاكَ بِهِ، وَفَضَّلَني عَلى كَثيرٍ مِمَّنْ خَلَقَ تَفْضيلا.

Alhamdu lillahil-lathee AAafanee mimmab-talaka bih, wafaddalanee AAala katheerin mimman khalaqa tafdeela.

'All praise is for Allah Who saved me from that which He tested you with and Who most certainly favoured me over much of His creation.'

---

78. REMEMBRANCE SAID AT A SITTING OR GATHERING...ETC

(185)

Ibn AAumar 🙵 *said: It would be counted that the Messenger of Allah* ﷺ *would say one hundred times at any one sitting before getting up:*

رَبِّ اغْفِرْ لي، وَتُبْ عَلَيَّ، إِنَّكَ أَنْتَ التَّوَّابُ الغَفور.

Rabbigh-fir lee watub AAalay, innaka antat-tawwabul-ghafoor.

'O my Lord, forgive me and turn towards me (to accept my repentance). Verily You are The Oft-Returning. The Oft-Forgiving.'

79. SUPPLICATION FOR THE EXPIATION OF SINS SAID AT THE CONCLUSION OF A SITTING OR GATHERING...ETC

(186)

سُبْحـانَكَ اللّهُمَّ وَبِحَمدِك، أَشْهَدُ أَنْ لا إِلهَ إِلاَّ أَنْتَ أَسْتَغْفِرُكَ وَأَتوبُ إِلَيْك.

Subhanakal-lahumma wabihamdik, ashhadu an la ilaha illa ant, astaghfiruka wa-atoobu ilayk.

'How perfect You are O Allah, and I praise You. I bear witness that None has the right to be worshipped except You. I seek Your forgiveness and turn to You in repentance.'

CONT.79. SUPPLICATION FOR CONCLUDING ALL SITTINGS

AAaishah رضي الله عنها *said: Whenever The Messenger of Allah* ﷺ *would betake a seat, read Quran or pray, he would always conclude it with certain words, I (i.e. AAaishah) said: O Messenger of Allah* ﷺ*, I have noticed that whenever you betake a seat, read Quran or pray, you always conclude it with these words. He said: Yes, whoever speaks good, it (i.e. the supplication) will be a seal for that goodness and whoever speaks ill, it will be an atonement for him.'*

سُبْحـانَكَ وَبِحَمدِكَ، لا إِلهَ إِلاّ أَنْتَ أَسْتَغْفِرُكَ وَأَتوبُ إِلَيْكَ.

Subhanaka wabihamdik, la ilaha illa anta astaghfiruka wa-atoobu ilayk.

'How perfect You are and I praise You. None has the right to be worshipped except You, I seek Your forgiveness and turn in repentance to You.'

80. RETURNING A SUPPLICATION OF FORGIVENESS

(188)

'AAabdullah Ibn Sarjis ﷺ *said: 'I went to see the Prophet* ﷺ *and ate from his food and then said to him:*

غَفَرَ اللهُ لَكَ يا رَسولَ اللهِ.

Ghafaral-lahu laka ya rasoolal-lah.

'May Allah forgive you, O Messenger of Allah.'
...he ﷺ replied:

وَلَكَ.

wa-lak

'and you.'

81. SUPPLICATION SAID TO ONE WHO DOES YOU A FAVOUR

(189)

'If someone does you a favour and you say:

$$\text{جَزَاكَ اللّٰهُ خَيْراً.}$$

Jazakal-lahu khayran.

'May Allah reward you with goodness.'
...then you have indeed excelled in praising him.'

82. PROTECTION FROM THE DAJJAL

-Dajjal: among the great signs of the last hour and the greatest trials to befall mankind, which every Prophet has warned about. Most of mankind will folow him. He will appear from Asbahan, Iran at the time when Muslims will conquer Constantinople. He will be given special powers and will make the truth seem false and vice versa. He will claim to be righteous and then he will claim prophet-hood and finally, divinity. From his features is that he will be blind in his right eye which is a definite proof that contradicts his claim to be Allah as it is a sign of imperfection. The word *Kafir* will be written between his eyes which every believer, literate or illiterate will recognise.

(190)

'Whoever memorises the first ten verses of soorat Al-Kahf will be protected from Dajjal.'

One should also seek refuge with Allāh from the tribulations of the Dajjāl after the last tashahhud in prayer.(Refer to supplications #55 & #56)

83. SUPPLICATION SAID TO ONE WHO PRONOUNCES HIS LOVE FOR YOU, FOR ALLAH'S SAKE

(191)

أَحَبَّكَ الَّذِي أَحْبَبْتَنِي لَه.

Aḥabbakal-lathee aḥbabtanee lah.

'May He, for whom you have loved me, love you.'

84. SUPPLICATION SAID TO ONE WHO HAS OFFERED YOU SOME OF HIS WEALTH

(192)

بَارَكَ اللهُ لَكَ فِي أَهْلِكَ وَمَالِك.

Barakal-lahu laka fee ahlika wamalik.

'May Allāh bless for you, your family and wealth.'

85. SUPPLICATION SAID TO THE DEBTOR WHEN HIS DEBT IS SETTLED

(193)

بَارَكَ اللهُ لَكَ فِي أَهْلِكَ وَمالِك، إِنَّمَا جَـزَاءُ السَّلَفِ الْحَمْدُ والأَدَاء.

Barakal-lahu laka fee ahlika wamalik, innama jaza-os-salafil-ḥamdu wal-ada/.

'May Allah bless for you, your family and wealth. Surely commendation and payment are the reward for a loan.'

86. SUPPLICATION FOR FEAR OF SHIRK

-shirk: to associate others with Allah in those things which are specific to Him. This can occur in (1) belief, e.g. to believe that other than Allah has the power to benefit or harm, (2) speech, e.g. to swear by other than Allah and (3) action, e.g. to bow or prostrate to other than Allah.

(194)

اللّٰهُمَّ إِنِّي أَعوذُبِكَ أَنْ أُشْرِكَ بِكَ وَأَنا أَعْلَمْ، وَأَسْتَغْفِرُكَ لِما لا أَعْلَمَ.

Allahumma innee aAAoothu bika an oshrika bika wa-ana aAAlam, wa-astaghfiruka lima la aAAlam.

'O Allah, I take refuge in You lest I should commit *shirk* with You knowingly and I seek Your forgiveness for what I do unknowingly.'

87. RETURNING A SUPPLICATION AFTER HAVING BESTOWED A GIFT OR CHARITY UPON SOMEONE

(195)

AAaishah رضي الله عنها reported that the Messenger of Allah ﷺ was given a sheep and he ordered for it's distribution. When the servant would come back (from distributing it), AAaishah would ask: 'What did they say?', he replied: They would supplicate:

بارَكَ اللهُ فيكُمْ.

Barakal-lahu feekum.

'May Allah bless you all.'
...AAaishah would then say:

وَفيهِـمْ بارَكَ الله.

Wafeehim barakal-lah.

'and may Allah bless them.'
...we return their supplication in a similar way and our
reward remains with us.

88. FORBIDDANCE OF ASCRIBING THINGS TO OMENS

This supplication is used whenever one initially thinks a casual event or occurrence to foretell good or evil, using it as a basis to determine which action he should undertake, but he then denounces such a link, relies on Allah and then says this supplication as an expiation for this act, since it falls under the category of *shirk*.

(196)

اللّهُمَّ لا طَيْرَ إلاَّ طَيْرُك، وَلا خَيْرَ إلاَّ خَيْرُك، وَلا إلهَ غَيْرُك.

Allahumma la tayra illa tayruk, wala khayra illa khayruk, wala ilaha ghayruk.

'O Allah, there is no omen but there is reliance on You, there is no good except Your good and none has the right to be worshipped except You.'

89. SUPPLICATION SAID WHEN MOUNTING AN ANIMAL OR ANY MEANS OF TRANSPORT

(197)

بِسْمِ اللهِ وَالْحَمْدُ للهِ، سُبْحانَ الّذي سَخَّرَ لَنا هذا وَما كُنّا لَهُ مُقْرِنِين، وَإِنّا إِلى رَبِّنا لَمُنقَلِبون، الْحَمْدُ للهِ، الْحَمْدُ للهِ، الْحَمْدُ للهِ، اللهُ أَكْبَر، اللهُ أَكْبَر، اللهُ أَكْبَر، سُبْحانَكَ اللّهُمَّ إِنّي ظَلَمْتُ نَفْسي فاغْفِرْ لي، فَإِنَّهُ لا يَغْفِرُ الذُّنوبَ إِلاّ أَنْت.

Bismil-lah, walhamdu lillah, subhanal-lathee sakhkhara lana hatha wama kunna lahu muqrineen, wainna ila rabbina lamunqaliboon, alhamdu lillah, alhamdu lillah, alhamdu lillah, Allahu akbar, Allahu akbar, Allahu akbar, subhanakal-lahumma innee _th_alamtu nafsee faghfir lee fainnahu la yaghfiruth-thunooba illa ant.

'In the name of Allah and all praise is for Allah. How perfect He is, the One Who has placed this (transport) at our service and we ourselves would not have been capable of that, and to our Lord is our final destiny. All praise is for Allah, All praise is for Allah, All praise is for Allah, Allah is the greatest, Allah is the greatest, Allah is the greatest. How perfect You are, O Allah, verily I have wronged my soul, so forgive me, for surely none can forgive sins except You.'

90. SUPPLICATION FOR TRAVEL

(198)

اللهُ أكبَر ، اللهُ أكبَر ، اللهُ أكبَر ، سُبْحانَ الَّذي سَخَّرَ لَنا هذا وَما كُنَّا لَهُ مُقْرِنين، وَإِنَّا إلى رَبِّنا لَمُنْقَلِبون، اللَّهُمَّ إِنَّا نَسْأَلُكَ في سَفَرِنا هذا البِرَّ والتَّقْوى، وَمِنَ الْعَمَلِ ما تَرْضى، اللَّهُمَّ هَوِّنْ عَلَينا سَفَرَنا هذا واطْوِ عَنّا بُعْدَه، اللَّهُمَّ أَنْتَ الصّاحِبُ في السَّفَر، وَالْخَليفَةُ في الأهلِ، اللَّهُمَّ إِنّي أَعوذُبِكَ مِنْ وَعْثاءِ السَّفَر، وَكَآبَةِ الْمَنْظَر، وَسوءِ الْمُنْقَلَبِ في المالِ وَالأَهْل.

Allahu akbar, Allahu akbar, Allahu akbar, subhanal-lathee sakhkhara lana hatha wama kunna lahu muqrineen, wa-inna ila rabbina lamunqaliboon, allahumma inna nas-aluka fee safarina hatha albirra wattaqwa, waminal-AAamali ma tarda, allahumma hawwin AAalayna safarana hatha, watwi AAanna buAAdah, allahumma antas-sahibu fis-safar, walkhaleefatu fil-ahl, allahumma innee aAAoothu bika min waAAtha-is-safar, waka-abatil-manthar, wasoo-il-munqalabi fil-mali wal-ahl.

'Allah is the greatest, Allah is the greatest, Allah is the greatest, How perfect He is, The One Who placed this (transport) at our service, and we ourselves would not have been capable of that, and to our Lord is our final destiny. O Allah, we ask You for *birr* and *taqwa* in this journey of ours, and we ask You for deeds which please You. O Allah, facilitate our journey and let us cover it's distance quickly. O Allah, You are The Companion on the journey and The Successor over the family, O Allah, I take refuge with You from the difficulties of travel, from having a change of hearts and being in a bad predicament, and I take refuge in You from an ill fated outcome with wealth and family.'

-*birr* and *taqwa*: two comprehensive terms which individually, refer to all good actions and obedience i.e. performing the commanded actions and avoiding the prohibited actions. When combined together, *birr* refers to doing those actions which have been commanded and *taqwa* refers to avoiding those actions which have been prohibited.

-*A successor*: one who succeeds another due to the latter's absence or death. This is the correct meaning of the word *khaleefah*; thus, it is incorrect to believe that Adam is the khaleefah (*vicegerent*, as is commonly translated) of Allah on earth because Allah is never absent, and will never die. This supplication proves the correct understanding of this term and shows that Allah succeeds us and guards whom we leave behind when we die or are absent.

…upon returning the same supplication is recited with the following addition:

آيِبُـونَ تائِبُـونَ عابِـدونَ لِرَبِّنا حامِـدون .

Ayiboona, ta-iboona, AAabidoona, lirabbina hamidoon.

'We return, repent, worship and praise our Lord.'

91. SUPPLICATION UPON ENTERING A TOWN OR VILLAGE…ETC
(199)

أَللَّهُمَّ رَبَّ السَّمواتِ السَّبْعِ وَما أَظْلَلَن، وَرَبَّ الأَراضينَ السَّبْعِ وَما أَقْلَلَن، وَرَبَّ الشَّياطينِ وَما أَضْلَلَن، وَرَبَّ الرِّياحِ وَما ذَرَيْن، أَسْأَلُكَ خَيْرَ هذِهِ الْقَرْيَةِ وَخَيْرَ أَهْلِها، وَخَيْرَ ما فيها، وَأَعوذُ بِكَ مِنْ شَرِّها وَشَرِّ أَهْلِها، وَشَرِّ ما فيها.

Allahumma rabbas-samawatis-sabAAi wama athlaln, warabbal-aradeenas-sabAAi wama aqlaln, warabbash-shayateeni wama adlaln, warabbar-riyahi wama tharayn, as-aluka khayra hathihil-qaryah, wakhayra ahlilha wakhayra ma feeha, wa-aAAoothu bika min sharriha washarri ahliha, washarri ma feeha.

'O Allah, Lord of the seven heavens and all that they envelop, Lord of the seven earths and all that they carry, Lord of the devils and all whom they misguide, Lord of the winds and all whom they whisk away. I ask You for the goodness of this village, the goodness of its inhabitants and for all the goodness found within it and I take refuge with You from the evil of this village, the evil of its inhabitants and from all the evil found within it.'

92. WHEN ENTERING THE MARKET
(200)

لا إلهَ إلاّ اللهُ وحدَهُ لا شريكَ لهُ، لهُ الْمُلْكُ ولهُ الحَمْدُ، يُحْيِي وَيُميتُ وَهُوَ حَيٌّ لا يَموت، بِيَدِهِ الخَيْرُ وَهوَ على كلّ شيءٍ قدير.

La ilaha illal-lah, wahdahu la shareeka lah, lahul-mulku walahul-hamd, yuhyee wayumeetu wahuwa hayyun la yamoot, biyadihil-khayru wahuwa AAala kulli shayin qadeer.

'None has the right to be worshipped except Allah, alone, without partner, to Him belongs all sovereignty and praise. He gives life and causes death, and He is living and does not die. In His hand is all good and He is over all things, omnipotent.'

93. SUPPLICATION FOR WHEN THE MOUNTED ANIMAL (OR MEAN OF TRANSPORT) STUMBLES

(201)

$$\text{بِسْمِ اللهِ .}$$

Bismil-lah.

'In the name of Allah.'

94. SUPPLICATION OF THE TRAVELLER FOR THE RESIDENT

(202)

$$\text{أَسْتَوْدِعُكُمُ اللَّهَ الَّذِي لا تَضِيعُ وَدائِعُهُ .}$$

AstawdiAAukumul-lah, allathee la tadeeAAu wada-iAAuh.

'I place you in the trust of Allah, whose trust is never misplaced.'

95. SUPPLICATION OF THE RESIDENT FOR THE TRAVELLER

(203)

أَسْتَوْدِعُ اللَّهَ دِينَكَ وَأَمَانَتَكَ، وَخَوَاتِيمَ عَمَلِكَ.

AstawdiAAul-laha deenak, wa-amanatak, wakhawateema AAamalik.

'I place your religion, your faithfulness and the ends of your deeds in the trust of Allah.'

(204)

زَوَّدَكَ اللَّهُ التَّقْوَى، وَغَفَرَ ذَنْبَكَ، وَيَسَّرَ لَكَ الْخَيْرَ حَيْثُمَا كُنْتَ.

Zawwadakal-lahut-taqwa, waghafara thanbak, wayassara lakal-khayra haythuma kunt.

'May Allah endow you with taqwa, forgive your sins and facilitate all good for you, wherever you be.'

-taqwa: a comprehensive term which refers to all good actions and obedience i.e. performing the commanded actions and avoiding the prohibited actions.

96. REMEMBRANCE WHILE ASCENDING OR DESCENDING

(205)

Jabir ﷺ said: While ascending, we would say:

اللَّهُ أَكْبَر.

Allahu akbar.

'Allah is the greatest.'

...and when descending, we would say:

سُبْحَانَ اللَّه.

Subhanal-lah.

'How perfect Allah is.'

97. PRAYER OF THE TRAVELLER AS DAWN APPROACHES

(206)

سَمِعَ سامِعُ بِحَمْدِ اللهِ وَحُسْنِ بَلائِهِ عَلَيْنا. رَبَّنا صاحِبْنا وَأَفْضِلْ عَلَيْنا عائِذاً بِاللهِ مِنَ النَّارِ.

SamiAAa samiAAun bihamdil-lahi wahusni bala-ihi AAalayna. Rabbana sahibna wa-afdil AAalayna AAa-ithan billahi minan-nar.

'May a witness, be witness to our praise of Allah for His favours and bounties upon us. Our Lord, protect us, show favour on us and deliver us from every evil. I take refuge in Allah from the fire.'

98. STOPPING OR LODGING SOMEWHERE

(207)

أَعـوذُ بِكَلِماتِ اللهِ التّامّاتِ مِنْ شَرِّ ما خَلَقَ.

aAAoothu bikalimatil-lahit-tammati min sharri ma khalaq.

'I take refuge in Allah's perfect words from the evil that He has created.'

99. WHILE RETURNING FROM TRAVEL

(208)

Ibn AAumar ⚘ reported that the Messenger of Allah ﷺ on return from a battle or from performing the pilgrimage would say at every high point:

ا للهُ أَكْبَرَ، ا للهُ أَكْبَرَ، ا للهُ أَكْبَرَ.

Allahu akbar, Allahu akbar, Allahu akbar.

'Allah is the greatest, Allah is the greatest, Allah is the greatest.'

...and then he would say:

لا إلهَ إلاَّ اللّهُ وَحْدَهُ لا شريكَ لهُ، لهُ المُلكُ ولهُ الحَمْد، وهُوَ على كُلّ شيءٍ قَدير، آيِبونَ تائِبونَ عابِدونَ لِرَبّنا حامِدون، صَدَقَ اللّهُ وَعْدَه، وَنَصَرَ عَبْدَه، وَهَزَمَ الأَحْزابَ وَحْدَه.

La ilaha illal-lahu wahdahu la shareeka lah, lahul-mulku walahul-hamd, wahuwa AAala kulli shay-in qadeer, ayiboona ta-iboon, AAabidoon, lirabbina hamidoon, sadaqal-lahu waAAdah, wanasara AAabdah, wahazamal-ahzaba wahdah.

'None has the right to be worshipped except Allah, alone, without partner.   To Him belongs all sovereignty and praise, and He is over all things omnipotent.   We return, repent, worship and praise our Lord.   Allah fulfilled His promise, aided His Servant, and single-handedly defeated the allies.'

100. WHAT TO SAY UPON RECEIVING PLEASING OR DISPLEASING NEWS
(209)

When he ﷺ used to receive pleasant news, he ﷺ would say:

الْحَمْدُ للّهِ الَّذي بِنِعْمَتِهِ تَتِمُّ الصّالِحات .

Alhamdu lillahil-lathee biniAAmatihi tatimmus-salihat.

'All Praise is for Allah by whose favour good works are accomplished.'

...and upon receiving displeasing news, he ﷺ would say:

الْحَمْدُ للهِ على كُلِّ حال.

Alḥamdu lill<u>a</u>hi AAal<u>a</u> kulli ḥal.

'All Praise is for All<u>a</u>h in all circumstances.'

101. EXCELLENCE OF SENDING PRAYERS UPON THE PROPHET ﷺ

(210)

The Prophet ﷺ said: 'Whoever sends a prayer upon me, Allah sends ten upon him.'

(211)

He ﷺ also said: 'Do not take my grave as a place of habitual ceremony. Send prayers upon me, for verily your prayers reach me wherever you are.'

(212)

He ﷺ also said: 'A miser is one whom when I am mentioned to him, fails to send prayers upon me.'

102. EXCELLENCE OF SPREADING THE ISLAMIC GREETING

(213)

The Messenger of All<u>a</u>h ﷺ said: 'You shall not enter paradise until you believe, and you shall not believe until you love one another. Shall I not inform you of something, if you were to act upon it, you will indeed achieve mutual love for one another? Spread the greeting amongst yourselves.'

(214)

AAamm*a*r ﷺ said: 'Three characteristics, whoever combines them, has completed his faith: to be just, to spread greetings to all people and to spend (charitably) out of the little you have.'

(215)

'AAabdull*a*h Ibn AAamr ﷺ reported that a man asked the Prophet ﷺ: 'Which Isl*a*m is the best?'. He ﷺ replied: Feed (the poor), and greet those whom you know as well as those whom you do not.'

103. SUPPLICATION SAID UPON HEARING A ROOSTER CROW OR THE BRAYING OF AN ASS

(216)

'If you hear the crow of a rooster, ask All*a*h for his bounty for it has seen an angel and if you hear the braying of an ass, seek refuge in All*a*h for it has seen a devil.'

104. SUPPLICATION UPON HEARING THE BARKING OF DOGS AT NIGHT

(217)

'If you hear the barking of dogs or the braying of asses at night, seek refuge in All*a*h for they see what you do not.'

105. SUPPLICATION SAID FOR ONE YOU HAVE INSULTED

(218)

اللهُمَّ فَأَيُّمَا مُؤْمِنٍ سَبَبْتُهُ فَاجْعَلْ ذَلِكَ لَهُ قُرْبَةً إِلِيكَ يَوْمَ القِيَامةِ.

All*a*humma fa-ayyum*a* mu/minin sababtuhu fajAAal *th*alika lahu qurbatan ilayka yawmal-qiy*a*mah.

'O Allah, to any believer whom I have insulted, let that be cause to draw him near to You on the Day of Resurrection.'

106. THE ETIQUETTE OF PRAISING A FELLOW MUSLIM

(219)

He ﷺ said: 'If anyone of you is impelled to praise his brother, then he should say: 'I deem so-and-so to be…and Allah is his reckoner…and I don't praise anyone, putting it (i.e. my praising) forward, in front of Allah's commendation, however I assume him so and so'…if he knows that of him.'

107. SUPPLICATION SAID BETWEEN THE YEMENI CORNER AND THE BLACK STONE (AT THE KAAABAH)

(220)

The Prophet ﷺ used to say between the Yemeni corner and the black stone:

﴿ رَبَّنَا آتِنَا فِي الدُّنْيَا حَسَنَةً وَفِي الآخِرَةِ حَسَنَةً وَقِنَا عَذَابَ النَّارِ ﴾

❮Rabbana atina fee alddunya hasanatan wafee al-akhirati hasanatan waqina AAathaba alnnar ❯
[Al-Baqarah: 201]

'O our Lord, grant us the best in this life and the best in the next life, and protect us from the punishment of the Fire.'

108. SUPPLICATION SAID WHEN AT MOUNT SAFA & MOUNT MARWAH

Jabir ﷺ *said when describing the Prophet's* ﷺ *pilgrimage:*
'…and when he approached mount Safa he recited:

﴾إِنَّ الصَّفَا وَالمَرْوَةَ مِنْ شَعَائِرِ اللهِ…﴿

❴Innas-safa wa-almarwata min shaAAa-iri Allah…❵

'Indeed Safa and Marwah are from the places of
worship of Allah…'

أَبْدَأُ بِمَا بَدَأَ اللهُ بِهِ.

Abda-o bima bada'al-lahu bih.

'I begin with what Allah began with.'

*…so he started with Safa and climed it until he could see
the KaAAbah, he then faced it and said:*

اللهُ أَكْبَرُ، اللهُ أَكْبَرُ، اللهُ أَكْبَرُ.

Allahu akbar, Allahu akbar, Allahu akbar.

'Allah is the greatest, Allah is the greatest, Allah is
the greatest.'

*…and then he would say the following three times making
a supplication (one should make a personal supplication)
after each time:*

لَا إِلَهَ إِلَّا اللهُ وَحْدَهُ لَا شَرِيكَ لَهُ، لَهُ المُلْكُ وَلَهُ الحَمْدُ وهُوَ عَلَى
كُلِّ شَيءٍ قَدِيرٌ، لَا إِلَهَ إِلَّا اللهُ وَحْدَهُ أَنْجَزَ وَعْدَهُ، وَنَصَرَ عَبْدَهُ
وَهَزَمَ الأَحْزَابَ وَحْدَهُ.

**La ilaha illal-lahu wahdahu la shareeka lah, lahul-
mulku walahul-hamd, wahuwa AAala kulli shayin
qadeer, la ilaha illal-lahu wahdah, anjaza**

waAAdah, wanasara AAabdah, wahazamal -ahzaba wahdah.

'None has the right to be worshipped except Allah, alone, without partner.To Him belongs all sovereignty and praise and He is over all things amnipotent. None has the right to be worshipped except Allah alone. He fulfilled His promise, aided His Servant and single-handedly defeated the allies.'

...he ﷺ would repeat this action at Marwah.

109. THE DAY OF AA'ARAFAH
(222)

'The best of supplications is the supplication on the day of AAarafah and the best which I and the Prophets before me have said (is):

لَا إِلَهَ إِلَّا اللهُ وَحْدَهُ لَا شَرِيكَ لَهُ، لَهُ المُلْكُ وَلَهُ الحَمْدُ وهُوَ عَلَى كُلِّ شَيْءٍ قَدِيرٌ.

La ilaha illal-lahu wahdahu la shareeka lah, lahul-mulku walahul-hamd, wahuwa AAala kulli shayin qadeer.

'None has the right to be worshipped except Allah, alone, without partner. To Him belongs all praise and sovereignty and He is over all things omnipotent.'

110. AT THE SACRED SITE (AL-MASHAAAR AL-HARAM)
(223)

Jabir ✿ said: 'He ﷺ *rode Al-Qaswa until he reached Al-MashAAar Al-Haram, he then faced the qiblah, supplicated to Allah, and extoled His greatness and oneness. He stood until the sun shone but left before it rose.'*

-Al-Qaswa: The name of the Prophet's ﷺ camel.

111. WHEN THROWING EACH PEBBLE AT THE JAMARAT

i.e. Stoning the three areas at Mina during Hajj.

(224)

Every time the Prophet ﷺ threw a pebble at any of the three jamarat, he would say:

اللهُ أَكْبَرُ.

Allahu akbar.

'Allah is the greatest'

…on completion of the first jamarah, he advanced a little, stood facing the qiblah, raised his hands and supplicated. He also did this after the second jamarah but not the third.'

112. AT THE BLACK STONE

(225)

'The Prophet ﷺ circled the KaAAbah on a camel, every time he reached the black stone he would point to it with his staff and say:

اللهُ أَكْبَرُ.

Allahu akbar

'Allah is the greatest'

113. SUPPLICATION MADE AGAINST AN ENEMY

(226)

اللَّهُمَّ مُنْزِلَ الكِتَابِ سَريعَ الحِسابِ اهْزِمَ الأَحْزَابَ اللَّهُمَّ اهْزِمْهُمْ وَزَلْزِلْهُمْ.

Allahumma munzilal-kitab, sareeAAal-hisab, ihzimil-ahzab, allahummah-zimhum wazalzilhum.

'O Allah, Revealer of the Book, Swift at reckoning, defeat the confederates. O Allah, defeat them and convulse them.'

114. WHAT TO SAY WHEN IN FEAR OF A PEOPLE

(227)

اللَّهُمَّ اكْفِنِيهِمْ بِما شِئْتَ.

Allahummak-fineehim bima shi/t.

'O Allah, protect me from them with what You choose.'

115. WHAT TO SAY AT TIMES OF AMAZEMENT AND DELIGHT

(228)

سُبْحَانَ اللهِ!

Subhanal-lah!.

'How perfect Allah is.'

(229)

اللهُ أَكْبَرُ!

Allahu akbar.

'Allah is the greatest.'

116. WHAT TO DO UPON RECEIVING PLEASANT NEWS

(230)

The Prophet ﷺ *would prostrate in gratitude to Allah upon receiving news which pleased him or which caused pleasure.*

117. WHAT TO SAY AND DO WHEN FEELING SOME PAIN IN THE BODY

(231)

'Place your hand at the site of the pain and say:

بِسْمِ اللهِ (ثَلاثاً)

Bismil-lah (three times)

'In the name of Allah' (three times)
…the supplicate seven times:

أَعُوذُ بِاللهِ وَقُدْرَتِهِ مَنْ شَرِّ مَا أَجِدُ وَأُحَاذِرُ. (سبع مرات)

aAAoothu billahi waqudratih min sharri ma ajidu wa-ohathir. (seven times).

'I take refuge in Allah and within His omnipotence from the evil that I feel and am wary of.' (seven times)

118. WHAT TO SAY WHEN IN FEAR OF AFFLICTING SOMETHING OR SOMEONE WITH ONE'S EYE

-The Evil Eye: To look at something and be impressed with it, causing harm to befall it. This "looking" *may or may not* involve jealousy, and can occur *unintentionally, indeed be part of a person's nature!* A person can even inflict harm *on himself.*

From the supplications for the protection against the Evil Eye:

اللّهُمَّ بارِك عَلَيه.

Allahumma barik AAalayh.

'O Allah, send blessing upon him.'

ما شاءَ اللّه، لا قُوَّةَ إلاّ بِاللّه.

Ma shaal-lah, la quwwata illa billah.

'(this is) that which Allah has willed, there is no power except with Allah.'

(232)
'If you see something from your brother, yourself or wealth which you find impressing, then invoke blessings for it, for the evil eye is indeed true'.

119. ETIQUETTE OF RETIRING FOR THE NIGHT
(233)
'When night falls (i.e. Al-Maghrib), restrain your children (from going out) because at such time the devils spread about. After a period of time has passed, let them be. Shut your doors and mention Allah's name, for verily the devil does not open a shut door, tie up your water-skins and mention Allah's name, cover your vessels with anything and mention Allah's name and put out your lamps.'

---

120. THE TALBIYAH

(234)

لَبَّيْكَ اللَّهُمَّ لَبَّيْكَ، لَبَّيْكَ لَا شَرِيكَ لَكَ لَبَّيْكَ، إِنَّ الْحَمْدَ وَالنِّعْمَةِ، لَكَ وَالْمُلْكُ، لَا شَرِيكَ لَكَ.

Labbaykal-lahumma labbayk, labbayka la shareeka laka labbayk, innal-hamda wanniAAmata laka walmulk, la shareeka lak.

'Here I am O Allah, (in response to Your call), here I am. Here I am, You have no partner, here I am. Verily all praise, grace and sovereignty belong to You. You have no partner.'

121. WHAT TO SAY WHEN STARTLED

(235)

لَا إِلَهَ إِلَّا اللّهُ.

La ilaha illal-lah.

'None has the right to be worshipped except Allah.'

122. WHAT IS SAID TO A KAFIR WHEN HE SNEEZES

(236)

يَهْدِيكُمُ اللّهُ وَيُصْلِحُ بَالَكُمْ.

Yahdeekum wayuslihu balakum.

'May Allah guide you and rectify your condition.'

123. RETURNING A GREETING TO A KAFIR

(237)

'When the people of the Book greet you, reply by saying:

وَعَلَيْكُمْ.

WaAAalaykum.

'And upon you.'

---

124. WHEN INSULTED WHILE FASTING
(238)

إِنِّي صَائِم، إِنِّي صَائِم.

Innee <u>sa</u>-im, innee <u>sa</u>-im.

'I am fasting, I am fasting.'

---

125. WHEN SLAUGHTERING OR OFFERING A SACRIFICE
(239)

بِسْمِ اللهِ واللهُ أَكْبَرُ اللَّهُمَّ مِنْكَ ولَكَ اللَّهُمَّ تَقَبَّلْ مِنِّي.

Bismil-l<u>a</u>h wall<u>a</u>hu akbar, all<u>a</u>humma minka walak, all<u>a</u>humma taqabbal minnee.

'In the name of All<u>a</u>h, and All<u>a</u>h is the greatest. O All<u>a</u>h, (it is) from You and belongs to You, O All<u>a</u>h, accept this from me.'

---

126. WHAT IS SAID TO WARD OFF THE DECEPTION OF THE OBSTINATE SHAY<u>TA</u>NS
(240)

أَعُوذُ بِكَلِمَاتِ اللهِ التَّامَّاتِ الَّتِي لَا يُجَاوِزُهُنَّ بِرٌّ وَلَا فَاجِرٌ مِنْ شَرِّ مَا خَلَقَ، وَبَرَأَ وَذَرَأَ، وِمِنْ شَرِّ مَا يَنْزِلُ مِنَ السَّمَاءِ وِمِنْ شَرِّ مَا

يَعْرُجُ فِيهَا، وَمِن شَرِّ مَا ذَرَأَ فِي الأَرْضِ وَمِنْ شَرِّ مَا يَخْرُجُ مِنْهَا، وَمِنْ شَرِّ فِتَنِ اللَّيْلِ وَالنَّهَارِ، وَمِنْ شَرِّ كُلِّ طَارِقٍ إِلَّا طَارِقاً يَطْرُقُ بِخَيْرٍ يَا رَحْمَانُ.

aAAoothu bikalimatil-lahit-tammat, allatee la yujawizu-hunna barrun wala fajir min sharri ma khalaq, wabaraa watharaa, wamin sharri ma yanzilu minas-sama/, wamin sharri ma yaAAruju feeha, wamin sharri ma tharaa fil-ard, wamin sharri ma yakhruju minha, wamin sharri fitnanil-layli wannahar, wamin sharri kulli tariqin illa tariqan yatruqu bikhayrin ya Rahman.

'I take refuge within Allah's perfect words which no righteous or unrighteous person can transgress, from all the evil that He has created, made and originated. (I take refuge) from the evil that descends from the sky and the evil that rises up to it. (I take refuge) from the evil that is spread on Earth and the evil that springs from her, and I take refuge from the evil of the tribulations of night and day, and the evil of one who visits at night except the one who brings good, O Merciful One.'

127. SEEKING FORGIVENESS AND REPENTANCE

(241)

The Messenger of Allah ﷺ said: 'By Allah, I seek forgiveness and repent to Allah, more than seventy times a day.'

(242)

He ﷺ also said: 'O People, Repent! Verily I repent to Allah, a hundred times a day.'

(243)

He ﷺ also said: 'Whoever says:

أَسْتَغْفِرُ اللّٰهَ الَّذِي لَا إِلَهَ إِلَّا هُوَ الْحَيُّ الْقَيُّوْمُ وأَتُوبُ إِلَيْهِ.

Astaghfirul-lahal-lathee la ilaha illa huwal-hayyul-qayyoomu wa-atoobu ilayh.

'I seek Allah's forgiveness, besides whom, none has the right to be worshipped except He, The Ever Living, The Self-Subsisting and Supporter of all, and I turn to Him in repentance.'

…Allah would forgive him even if he was one who fled during the advance of an army.'

(244)

He ﷺ said: 'The nearest the Lord comes to His servant is in the middle of the night, so if you are able to be of those who remember Allah at that time, then be so.'

(245)

He ﷺ also said: 'The nearest a servant is to his Lord is when he is prostrating, so supplicate much therein.'

(246)

He ﷺ also said: 'verily my heart becomes preoccupied, and verily I seek Allah's forgiveness a hundred times a day.'

-preoccupied: i.e. in a state of *'forgetfulness'*. The Prophet ﷺ always used to increase in his remembrance of his Lord, in attaining a nearness to Allah and having consciousness of Allah to the extent that if this intensity lessened in anyway, he would regard it as a sin and would then race to seek forgiveness from Allah.

128. EXCELLENCE OF REMEMBRANCE AND GLORIFICATION OF ALLAH

(247)

Abu Hurayrah ﷺ *reported that the Messenger of Allah* ﷺ *said: 'Whoever says:*

لَا إِلٰهَ إِلَّا اللّٰهُ وَحْدَهُ لَا شَرِيكَ لَهُ، لَهُ الْمُلْكُ وَلَهُ الْحَمْد، وهُوَ

عَلَى كُلِّ شَيءٍ قَدِيرٌ. (مائة مرة).

La ilaha illal-lahu wahdahu la shareeka lah, lahul-mulku walahul-hamd, wahuwa AAala kulli shayin qadeer. (one hundred times)

'None has the right to be worshipped except Allah, alone, without partner. To Him belongs all sovereignty and praise and He is over all things omnipotent.'

...a hundred times during the day, has the reward of freeing ten slaves, a hundred good deeds are recorded for him and a hundred bad deeds are wiped away and he has gained refuge from the devil that day until evening and none shall come with anything better except someone who has done more.'

(248)

'Whoever says:

سُبْحَانَ اللّٰهِ وَبِحَمْدِهِ. (مائة مرة في اليوم)

Subhanal-lahi wabihamdih. (one hundred times daily)

'How perfect Allah is and I praise Him.'
...a hundred times during the day, his sins are wiped away, even if they are like the foam of the sea.'

(249)

Abu Hurayrah ؓ reported that the Messenger of Allah ﷺ said: 'Whoever says at morning and evening time:

سُبْحَانَ اللّٰهِ وَبِحَمْدِهِ (حين يصبح وحين يمسي)

Subhanal-lahi wabihamdih. (at morning & evening time)

'How perfect Allah is and I praise Him.'
...one hundred times, none shall come on the Day of Resurrection with anything better except someone who has said the same or even more.'

-morning: after prayer until the sunrises, **evening:** after AAasr prayer until the sunsets, however some scholars say: after the sunsets and onwards.

(250)

Aboo Ayyoob Al-Ansaree ؓ related that The Prophet ﷺ said: 'Whoever says:

لَا إِلٰهَ إِلَّا اللّٰهُ وَحْدَهُ لَا شَرِيكَ لَهُ، لَهُ المُلْكُ وَلَهُ الحَمْدُ وهُوَ عَلى كُلِّ شَيءٍ قَديرٌ.

La ilaha illal-lahu wahdahu la shareeka lah, lahul-mulku walahul-hamd, wahuwa AAala kulli shayin qadeer.

'None has the right to be worshipped except Allah, alone, without partener. To Him belongs all sovereignty and praise and He is over all things omnipotent.'

.....ten times is like one who has freed four souls from among the children of IsmaAAeel.'

(251)

Aboo Hurayrah ﷺ reported that the Messenger of Allah ﷺ said:'(There are) Two words, (which are) light on the tongue, heavy on the Scale and beloved to The Most Gracious:

سُبْحَانَ اللهِ وَبِحَمْدِهِ وسُبْحَانَ اللهِ العَظِيمِ .

Subhanal-lahi wabihamdih, wasubhanal-lahil-AAatheem.

' How perfect Allah is and I praise Him. How perfect Allah is, The Supreme.'

(252)

Aboo Hurayrah ﷺ reported that the Messenger of Allah ﷺ said: 'Saying:

سُبْحَانَ اللهِ، والحَمْدُ لله، لَا إِلَهَ إِلَّا اللهُ واللهُ أَكْبَرُ.

Subhanal-lah, walhamdu lillah, la ilaha illal-lah wallahu akbar.

' How perfect Allah is, and all praise is for Allah. None has the right to be worshipped except Allah, and Allah is the greatest.'

..... is more beloved to me than everything the sun has risen over.'

(253)

Sa'd ﷺ said: 'We were sitting with the Messenger of Allah ﷺ, and he said: 'Are any of you unable to gain a thousand good deeds each day?' Somebody then asked him ﷺ : How does one achieve a thousand good deeds? He replied: 'He should say:

$$\text{سُبْحَانَ اللهِ.}$$

Subhanal-lah.

'How perfect Allah is.'

....one hundred times, for a thousand good deeds are recorded for him or a thousand bad deeds are wiped away.'

(254)

Jabbir ﷺ related that the Prophet ﷺ said: 'Whoever says:

$$\text{سُبْحَانَ اللهِ العَظِيمِ وبِحَمْدِهِ.}$$

Subhanal-lahil-AAatheemi wabihamdih.

' How perfect Allah is . The Supreme, and I praise Him.'

.....a palm tree is planted for him in paradise.'

(255)

'AAabdullah Ibn Qays ﷺ related that the Prophet ﷺ said to him: ' O 'AAabdullah Ibn Qays, shall I not inform you of a treasure from the treasures of paradise?' He ﷺ then said: 'Say:

$$\text{لَا حَوِلَ وَلَا قُوَّةَ إِلَّا بِاللهِ.}$$

La hawla wala quwwata illa billah.

'There is no might nor power except with Allah.'

(256)

' the most beloved words to Allah are four:

سُبْحَانَ اللهِ، وَالْحَمْدُ لِلّهِ، وَلَا إِلَهَ إِلَّا اللهُ وَاللهُ أَكْبَرُ.

Subhanal-lah, walhamdu lillah, wala ilaha illal-lah, wallahu akbar.

' How perfect Allah is, all praise is for Allah. None has the right to be worshipped except Allah and Allah is the greatest.'

....it does not matter which of them you start with.'

(257)

SaAAd Ibn Abee Waqqas ﷺ narrated that a man came to the Messenger of Allah ﷺ and said to him: 'Teach me something which I should say?' He said: 'Say:

لَا إِلَهَ إِلَّا اللهُ وَحْدَهُ لَا شَرِيكَ لَهُ، اللهُ أَكْبَرُ كَبِيراً والْحَمْدُ لِلّهِ كَثِيراً، سُبْحَانَ اللهِ رَبِّ العَالَمِينَ، لَا حَوْلَ وَلَا قُوَّةَ إِلَّا بِاللهِ العَزِيزِ الْحَكِيمِ.

La ilaha illal-lah, wahdahu la shareeka lah, Allahu akbaru kabeera, walhamdu lillahi katheera, subhanal-lahi rabbil-AAalameen, la hawla wala quwwata illa billahil-AAazeezil-hakeem.

'None has the right to be worshipped except Allah, alone without partener. Allah is most great and much praise is for Allah. How perfect Allah is, Lord of the worlds. There is no might nor power except with Allah, The Exalted in might, The Wise.'

...the man then said: 'These are for my Lord, and what is for me?' He ﷺ replied:

'*Say:*

اللَّهُمَّ اغْفِرْ لِي، وَارْحَمْنِي، وَاهْدِنِي، وَارْزُقْنِي.

Allahummagh-fir lee, warhamnee, wahdinee, warzuqnee.

'O Allah, forgive me, have mercy upon me, guide me and grant me sustenance.'

(258)

Tariq Al-AshjaAAee ﷺ *said: 'When someone would embrace Islam, the Prophet* ﷺ *would teach him how to perform prayer and then order him to supplicate with the following words:*

اللَّهُمَّ اغْفِرْ لِي، وَارْحَمْنِي، وَاهْدِنِي، وَعَافِنِي وَارْزُقْنِي.

Allahummagh-fir lee, warhamnee, wahdinee, waAAafinee warzuqnee.

'O Allah, forgive me, have mercy upon me, guide me, give me health and grant me sustenance.'

(259)

Jabir Ibn 'AAabdullah ﷺ *related that the Messenger of Allah* ﷺ *said: 'Verily, the best supplication is:*

الْحَمْدُ لِلَّهِ.

Alhamdu lillah

'All praise is for Allah.'
…and indeed, the best form of remembrance is:

لَا إِلَهَ إِلَّا اللهُ.

La ilaha illal-lah.

'None has the right to be worshipped except Allah.'

---

(260)

'The everlasting righteous deeds:

سُبْحَانَ اللهِ، وَالْحَمْدُ لِلّٰهِ، لَا إِلٰهَ إِلَّا اللهُ وَاللهُ أَكْبَرُ وَلَا حَوْلَ وَلَا قُوَّةَ إِلَّا بِاللهِ.

Subhanal-lah, walhamdu lillah, la ilaha illal-lah, wallahu akbar, wala hawla wala quwwwata illa billah.

'How perfect Allah is, and all praise is for Allah. None has the right to be worshipped except Allah, and Allah is the greatest. There is no might nor power except with Allah.'

129. HOW THE PROPHET ﷺ MADE TASBEEH

Tasbeeh, it means here, to say:
Subhanal-lah, alhamdu lillah, Allahu akbar.

(261)

'AAabdullah Ibn AAamr ﷺ said: 'I saw the prophet ﷺ make tasbeeh with his right hand.'

ॐ ৪০ ॐ ৪০

O Allah, send peace and blessings upon our Prophet Muhammad ﷺ , his companions, and his family and all those who follow them in righteousness till the Day of Reckoning.

Ameen.

ॐ ৪০ ॐ ৪০

Invocations & supplications within this book

01- When waking up	5
02- Supplication when wearing a garment	6
03- Supplication said when wearing a new garment	7
04- Supplication said to someone wearing a new garment	7
05- Before undressing	8
06- Before entering the toilet	8
07- After leaving the toilet	9
08- When starting ablution	9
09- Upon completing the ablution	9
10- When leaving the home	10
11- Upon entering the home	11
12- Supplication when going to the mosque	11
13- Upon entering the mosque	12
14- Upon leaving the mosque	13
15- Supplications related to the athan	13
16- Supplication at the start of the prayer	15
17- While bowing in prayer (rukooAA)	22
18- Upon rising from the bowing position	23
19- Supplication whilst prostrating (sujood)	25
20- Supplication between the two prostrations	27
21- Supplication when prostrating due to recitation of the Quran	28
22- The Tashahhud	29
23- Prayers upon the Prophet ﷺ after the tashahhud	30
24- Supplication said after the last tashahhud and before salam	31
25- Remembrance after salam	39
26- Supplication for seeking guidance in forming a decision...	43
27- Remembrance said in the morning and evening	45
28- Remembrance before sleeping	57
29- Supplication when turning over during the night	64
30- Upon experiencing unrest, fear, apprehensiveness...	65
31- Upon seeing a good dream or a bad dream	65
32- Qunoot Al-Witr	66
33- Remembrance immediately after salam of the witr prayer	68
34- Supplication for anxiety and sorrow	69
35- Supplication for one in distress	71
36- Upon encountering an enemy or those of authority	72
37- Supplication for one afflicted with doubt in his faith	73
38- Settling a debt	74
39- Supplication for one afflicated by whisperings in prayer/recitation	75
40- Supplication for one whose affairs have become difficult	75

41- Upon committing a sin	76
42- Supplication for expelling the devil and his whisperings	76
43- Supplication when stricken with a mishap/overtaken by an affair	77
44- Placing childen under Allah's protection	77
45- When visiting the sick	78
46- Excellence of visiting the sick	79
47- Supplication of the sick who have renounced all hope of life	79
48- Instruction for the one nearing death	80
49- Supplication for one afflicted by a calamity	81
50- When closing the eyes of the deceased	81
51- Supplication for the deceased at the funeral prayer	82
52- Supplication for the advancement of reward during the funeral…	85
53- Condolence 66	86
54- Placing the deceased in the grave	87
55- After burying the deceased	87
56- Visiting the graves	88
57- Prayer said during a wind storm	88
58- Supplication upon hearing thunder	89
59- Supplication for rain 68	89
60- Supplication said when it rains	90
61- After rainfall	90
62- Asking for clear skies	91
63- Upon sighting the crescent moon	91
64- Upon breaking fast	91
65- Supplication before eating	92
66- Upon completing the meal	93
67- Supplication of the guest for the host	94
68- Supplication said to one offering a drink or intended to do that	94
69- Supplication said when breaking fast in someone's home	95
70- Supplication said by one fasting when presented with food…	95
71- Supplication said upon seeing the early or premature fruit	95
72- Supplication said upon sneezing	96
73- Supplication said to the newlywed	97
74- The groom's supplication on the wedding night…	97
75- Supplication before sexual intercourse	97
76- When angry	98
77- Supplication said upon seeing someone in trial or tribulation	98
78- Remembrance said at a sitting or gathering…etc	99
79- Supplication for the expiation of sins said at the conclusion of a sitting	99
Cont 79- Supplication for concluding all sittings	99
80- Returning a supplication of forgiveness	100
81- Supplication said to one who does you a favour	101
82- Protection from the Dajjal	101

83- What is said to one who pronounces his love for you, for Allah's sake	102
84- Supplication said to one who has offered you some of his wealth	102
85- Supplication said to the debtor when his debt is settled	102
86- Supplication for fear of shirk	103
87- Returning a supplication after having bestowed a gift/charity...	103
88- Forbiddance of ascribing things to omens	104
89- What is said when mounting an animal or any means of transport	105
90- Supplication for travel	105
91- Supplication upon entering a town or village...etc	107
92- When entering the market	108
93- Supplication for when the mounted animal stumbles	109
94- Supplication of the traveller for the resident	109
95- Supplication of the resident for the traveller	109
96- Remembrance while ascending or descending	110
97- Prayer of the traveller as dawn approaches	111
98- Stopping or lodging somewhere	111
99- While returning from travel	111
100- What to say upon receiving pleasing or displeasing news	112
101- Excellence of sending prayers upon the Prophet	113
102- Excellence of spreading the Islamic greeting	113
103- What is said upon hearing a rooster crow or the braying of an ass	114
104- Supplication upon hearing the barking of dogs at night	114
105- Supplication said for one you have insulted	114
106- The etiquette of praising a fellow Muslim	115
107- Supplication between the Yemeni corner and the black stone	115
108- Supplication said when at Mount Safa & Mount Marwah	115
109- The Day of Aaarafah	117
110- At the Sacred Site (Al-MashAAar Al-Haram)	117
111- When throwing each pebble at the Jamarat	118
112- At the black stone	118
113- Supplication made against an enemy	119
114- What to say when in fear of a people	119
115- What to say at times of amazement and delight	119
116- What to do upon receiving pleasant news	120
117- What to say and do when feeling some pain in the body	120
118- When in fear of afflicting something or someone with one's eye	120
119- Etiquette of retiring for the night	121
120- The Talbiyah	122
121- What to say when startled	122
122- What is said to a Kafir when he sneezes	122
123- Returning a greeting to a Kafir	122
124- When insulted while fasting	123
125- When slaughtering or offering a sacrifice	123

126- What is said to ward off the deception of the Obstinate Shaytans	123
127- Seeking forgiveness and repentance	124
128- Excellence of remembrance and glorification of Allah	126
129- How the prophet ﷺ made tasbeeh	132

Made in United States
Orlando, FL
29 November 2024

54663845R00076